TAKE THE PAIN

OUT OF PAINTING

-INTERIORS-

Glenn Haege

America's Master Handyman (TM)

Edited by Kathy Stief
Illustrated by Ken Taylor
Cover and Introduction Photos
by Edward R. Noble
Back Cover Photo by Gilbert Ecks

MASTER HANDYMAN PRESS, INC.

TAKE THE PAIN OUT OF PAINTING -INTERIORS-

Glenn Haege
America's Master Handyman(TM)

Edited by Kathy Stief

Published by:
  Master Handyman Press, Inc.
  Post Office Box 1498
  Royal Oak, MI 48068-1498

First Printing 1993

Printed in the United States of America

Library of Congress Cataloging in Publication Data.

Haege, Glenn
  How to take the pain out of painting: interiors.
  Bibliography: h.

ISBN 1- 880615-12-6

To Barbara, Eric and Heather with love.

Acknowledgments

My very special thanks go to Gerry Grass and Pat O'Malley. When I was young and green, these two very special people took the time to make sure I learned the real facts of Paint Product Knowledge. I can only hope that you have trainers as caring.

I was building a house while trying to write this book. It wouldn't have gotten done if my lovely wife Barbara had not spent a large part of her time getting me to sit down and write, even though I was distracted by a thousand other things. My great kids, Eric and Heather, also went out of their way to help.

The staff and management at WXYT Detroit, AM 1270, one of the nation's top "Talkers" did everything possible to support me in this effort. Jerry Baker, Rob David, Homer Formby, Joe Gagnon, Leonard Schwartz, Robert Senior and many others gave freely of their special knowledge.

Ken Taylor, one of the country's most sought after commercial artists, sacrificed his sleep on many nights because it was the only way to get the book out on time. This kind of extra effort and professionalism is all too often not recognized or appreciated. Thanks Ken.

Kathy Stief, a great lady, my editor, and friend, worked through many difficulties to make this book the best it could be.

Bill Damman, my friend and senior vice president of one of the nation's most respected, family-owned, hardware store chains, kept urging me on and gave me the support of his organization, because he felt this was a book his customers needed.

Equal thanks must go to Walter J. Gozdan, Technical Director of the Rohm and Haas Paint Quality Institute. Walter gave me carte blanche to use the vast resources of that great organization. Virtually everyone in both the paint and hardware industries only had to hear I had a problem, to come forward with possible solutions. Much that is right in this book should be credited to them. Any unseen errors, I did on my own.

As always, my final thanks has to go to my great listeners. Without you folks this book would not be possible. Enjoy.

Glenn Haege
Royal Oak, Michigan

TABLE OF CONTENTS

SUBJECT   PAGE

TABLE OF CONTENTS

SUBJECT   PAGE

TABLE OF CONTENTS

SUBJECT   PAGE

TABLE OF CONTENTS

SUBJECT   PAGE

TABLE OF CONTENTS

SUBJECT   PAGE

TABLE OF CONTENTS

SUBJECT   PAGE

INTRODUCTION

INTRODUCTION

Glenn Haege on location for his upcoming book, *TAKE THE PAIN OUT OF PAINTING! -EXTERIORS-*.

Painting is very important. You, the Do-It-Yourselfer, have made it second only to gardening, as the most popular DIY project in America.

There are many good reasons for this.

PAINTING IS:

1   **Definitely do-able.** This book gives you all   the information you need to do a masterful job.   It is something that you can do well and of which you can be very proud, no matter how old or young you are.

2   **The quickest way to change the personality of a house.**

3   **The fastest way to make your house express your personality.**

INTRODUCTION

4   The most economical way to brighten
and revive an older home.

5   The best investment you can make if you
are trying to sell your house.

6   A real bargain. The paints and coatings
of today are great improvements over paints available just
five years ago yet have increased very little in price.

7   A great Ego Builder. You see immediate
positive results. Other people come in, see, and
compliment the change immediately. You have
earned full bragging rights.

The paint manufacturers have heard your demand
for quality, economy, and ease of use. They are spending
vast sums in research and using advanced production
techniques and huge production runs to keep prices low.

When I recommend that you pay extra for a premium
paint, you can be sure that the improved quality is such that
you get far more performance than you are paying for.

This book is different from most other painting books
because it is laid out from the point of view of the Do-It-
Yourselfer, not the paint company or the painting
professional.

It covers almost every problem you can have with
interior painting and staining.

If you are a painting retailer, you will find this book is
written in simple terms and has all the real world
information you and your employees need to help your

INTRODUCTION

painting customers.

Most of this book is laid out on a project by project basis. If all you want to do is paint the living room, there's no need to learn how to paint kitchen cabinets.

When I first wrote this book, the first two, very long chapters were on paint and painting tools. Barb and the kids fell asleep reading those chapters.

I figured that you would probably fall asleep also. To keep the book more active, I cut these chapters down to a bare minimum.

In the present format you, the reader, should be able to take the book and say, *"OK, I'm going to paint the bathroom. Now, here's a chapter on how to paint the bathroom."*

Using this abbreviated approach, you should be able to sit down, read and absorb all the special problems you may run into painting the bathroom.

Every chapter includes many little project headings which describe what we want the project to look like when we're done. We then describe how to get there as fast and as easily as possible. An example of the kind of project description you'll find is:

"I want to paint the paneling to make the walls look lighter, and more uniform in color."

This description won't win any literary awards, but it shows exactly what that segment would be about. By the way, it's a good summary of what most people want when

INTRODUCTION

they paint the paneling in their den, breezeway or recreation room. If they don't want to change their paneling, just revive it, that would not be covered in this book.

The segment will then go on to show you step by step what you should do to accomplish that particular project. It will give you all the little tips you need to stop problems such as blotchy appearance, bleeding, shadowing, adhesion, chip resistance, etc.

"I'm going to paint my kitchen cabinets. They're formica, or they're wood. Or they're laminates of some kind." And, **"I want to paint over the Wallpaper,"** are examples of other project headings.

In each one, we begin with the project, the final result, and then go all the way back to the prep, and take you step by step to the final, successful conclusion.

A majority of the paints, tools, and other products called for , are made by many different suppliers. If there are many different products that do the same thing, we will use generic terms, not product names.

However, whenever a product is unique, or there are only one or two products that really do the job, brand names will be used.

Many definitions for words I use, as well as technical terms the professionals use, are in a glossary in the back. You'll also find sections on Stain Kills and color coordination in the Appendices.

INTRODUCTION

Anyone who knows me, knows that my favorite price is "free." A listing of free or inexpensive brochure names, companies and addresses, magazines and books is also included at the back of the book.

One thing this book is not.. It is not a refinishing book. You won't find anything about painting, varnishing or staining furniture, or hard wood floors. That's refinishing, and will be the subject of a later book.

PAINTING CONTRACTOR
VS.
DO-IT-YOURSELF

The following may sound like I am against painting contractors. I am not. It may also sound like I am lumping all painting contractors together.

Right from the start, I want to say no two painting contractors are exactly alike. Painters are, for the most part, highly skilled professionals. They do an excellent job considering the time and cost restraints under which they work.

I don't want to teach you to paint like a professional painter, because...

You, the Do-It-Yourselfer, can afford to do a much better job.

You, the Home-Owner / Do-It-Yourselfer, are operating from a completely different perspective.

INTRODUCTION

Time is money. Most painting jobs are let on a cost bid basis. If a painting contractor bid a job figuring in the time required for proper cleaning, preparation and the best possible paint, he would lose the job.

The professional painter is not in love with your house. All he wants to do is get in, and get out as quickly and inexpensively as possible. He doesn't want to "waste" time on wall washing and surface prep.(preparation).

Surface prep is the most important part of the job, and can easily double the life of your painting project. It can even eliminate the need to repaint (A painting contractor doesn't want that either).

The contractor usually wants to use the least expensive paint that will do the job, because paint cost comes out of his profits. You want the best paint for each project, because it greatly extends the beauty and service life of the job.

He wants maximum spread rate so he gets maximum coverage for his money and increases profits. You want maximum protection and beauty for your money.

The pro wants to make the job as simple as possible and will gladly paint the whole house a uniform white, just so that he gets out quicker. You want to save time, too. But you want the paint you select to compliment your decorating tastes and life style.

INTRODUCTION

BREAKDOWN OF PAINTING CONTRACTOR JOB COST

According to the Rohm and Haas Paint Quality Institute, up to 85% of the cost of a paint job is labor. If you do the job yourself, you are saving so much on the job, you can afford the highest quality paint and really do the job right.

85% Labor ▶ 15% Paint

Source: The Rohm and Haas Paint Quality Institute

UP TO 85 PERCENT of the cost of painting is for the contractor's labor, only 15 percent for paint. So, it pays to spend a few dollars more on long-lasting paint to avoid frequent re-painting. Top quality acrylic latex paint lasts 10 years or more, compared to three or four years for ordinary paint, says the Rohm and Haas Paint Quality Institute. In the end, better quality paint is far less expensive. *3573127*

INTRODUCTION

TIME ALLOCATION FOR THE AVERAGE PAINTING JOB

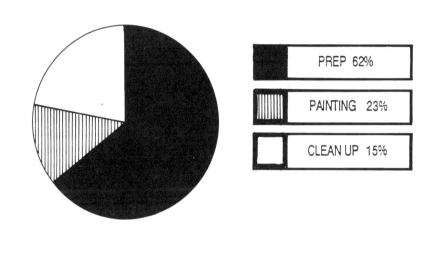

PREP 62%

PAINTING 23%

CLEAN UP 15%

ONLY 23% OF THE TIME ON THE AVERAGE PAINT JOB IS SPENT PAINTING. 77% IS SPENT IN PREPARATION AND CLEANUP. KITCHENS, BATHS, BASEMENTS OR EXTERIOR SIDING MAY CALL FOR EVEN MORE TIME OR PREP.

Using two coats of the highest quality paint, means that the job will look twice as good, twice as long, and give double the protection.

INTRODUCTION

Many painting contractors are really paint application professionals. They are most interested in the painting portion of the job for two reasons.

1   Painting is the part of the job on which they can make the most money.

2   It is usually the only portion of the job for which you, the homeowner, are willing to pay.

Remember: TIME IS MONEY. You can't expect a painting contractor to do two thirds of the work for free. If you use a painting contractor, demand the proper preparation. Get a separate quote on the prep. Your contractor deserves the money. You deserve the job done right.

How do you make certain that you are getting a good painting contractor?

As I always say, your check book is the most important tool in the tool box. Hiring a good painting contractor is your most important task. Here are the steps necessary to getting a good contractor:

1   Naturally, you start by asking your friends and relatives if they had some painting done recently.

2   Go to your favorite paint, hardware and home center stores and ask the store manager or owner which contractors they would recommend for your particular project. They will be delighted to tell you. The painters they recommend buy hundreds of gallons of paint from them every year, and they are delighted to return the favor.

INTRODUCTION

Just as important, they want you to get a good, professional contractor, so that you get a good job, and like their paint.

Each store will give you two or three references.

3   While you are at the store, get knowledgeable about paint. Bring your measurements, see approximately how much paint you will need. What does the paint store, or paint department manager say is the best paint for your particular job?

4   Call all the painting contractors and have them stop by your house for an appointment. Do not ask for a phone quote. Unless they can see the job, they can not quote it.

5   When the painting contractors come over for their appointment, tell them up front that you will want the quote in writing and that you will not sign anything that night.

6   Walk with them while they inspect the area to be painted. Give them all the information they need.

7   Tell them you require that their quote be in writing. You need them to specify exactly what preparation they are going to be responsible for. You want to know exactly what they are going to do.

Have them specify the paint they are going to use in writing. How many coats? This is an excellent time to talk paint quality. You don't care which brand paint they use, you demand that it be top of the line.

INTRODUCTION

Ask them about their guarantee. Exactly how long is this paint job guaranteed to last without being worn looking.

Will the paint job be scrubbable? Does he guarantee it?

8   Check out the contractors "bragging rights" (references) big time. Ask for at least five or ten people who got the same type of job you are getting. Get some names from this year, last year, two or three years ago. Make certain that you get their names, addresses and phone numbers.

Call all the references on the phone, then go to see them. They will be pleased as punch to recommend a good painter.

9   After you have gotten all your price quotes and checked all the references, one painter will be head and shoulders above the rest. Give him the contract.

10   You should require that the written contract specify an exact description of the area to be painted, exactly what prep will be done, type of paint to be used (Exact name, not just Sherwin Williams or Pittsburgh Paint, but the exact brand name from the can, along with its number and color identification.

11   Payment terms should be no more than 20% down. Stage payments are OK. However, there should be at least 20% to be paid upon completion, after you have inspected the job and made certain that clean up, as well as painting , was to your approval.

INTRODUCTION

12   Return the compliment. Contractors are just like you and me, they work hard trying to make a living. When you get a good job done, praise the contractor highly. Recommend him or her to your friends, neighbors and relatives.

When you do this, you are not just being a good person. What goes around, comes around. The customer who is loud in his praise and long in his recommendations, becomes a highly valued customer.

If you need service in the future, or a quote on another job, your contractor will bend over backward to give you that service and make a good quote.

That being said, let's stop talking and start doing.

Glenn Haege
America's Master Handyman

10/19/92

FOREWORD

Glenn Haege Is Must Reading.

For anyone who is a loyal listener to Glenn Haege every weekend in Detroit, this book is must reading. For anyone who has yet to discover Glenn Haege, this is a book that has more information on how to survive as a homeowner than just about anything in the world.

If you own a hammer and a screwdriver, the third thing you want in your toolbox is Glenn Haege's latest book.

Glenn Haege's new book combines his wit and wisdom, along with some of the best tips for homeowners that are found anywhere.

I can't think of a better gift for anyone.

Keith Crain
Publisher & Editorial Director,
Automotive News
Publisher, *Crain's Detroit Business*

You Need This Book on Your Work Bench.

I've been after Glenn to write this painting book for years. The reasons are simple. My customers need this book. My employees need this book. I need this book. If you paint, or if you are in any way associated with the painting or hardware industries, you need this book.

Glenn lists every different kind of painting problem (read opportunity) and gives easy to follow, step by step instructions. He not only tells how to solve the problem, but actually makes it sound like fun.

Surface preparation, Kitchens and Baths, and Basements present problems, so Glenn gives each a special chapter.

He also goes into the newly re-discovered *Faux Finish* painting techniques and gives simple instructions on how to do each one.

Glenn takes away the mystery from stain kills. He lists the proper kind of stain kill to solve every different kind of painting problem.

If you read, if you paint, and want to do it right, take my advice and give this book a permanent place on your work bench.

Great going Glenn!

Bill Damman, Sr. Vice President
Damman Hardware
Madison Heights, Michigan 48071

WARNING - DISCLAIMER

This book is designed to provide general painting information for the home handyman and woman. It is sold with the understanding that the publisher and author are not engaged in rendering legal, or other professional services. If expert assistance is required, the services of competent professionals should be sought.

Every effort has been made to make this text as complete and accurate as possible, and to assure proper credit is given to various contributors and manufacturers, etc. However, there may be mistakes, both typographical and in content. Therefore, this text should be used only as a general guide and not as the ultimate source of information. Furthermore, this book contains information current only up to the date of printing.

The purpose of this book is to educate and entertain. The author and Master Handyman Press Inc. shall have neither liability nor responsibility to any person or entity with respect to any loss or damage caused directly or indirectly by the information contained in this book.

WARNING - DISCLAIMER

PAINTS

Chapter I

PAINTS

Paint is the biggest bang for the buck in Remodeling.

Paint is a real bargain. Its value has not eroded through inflation. Quality remaining constant, the price of paint has not increased in the past 20 years.

The reason it is so economical is that the paint industry is highly competitive. The leading companies have chosen to use their technological improvements and production innovations to keep the price of paint down, the value up. This is a big plus for you, the consumer.

Painting is definitely the biggest change you can give a room, or the whole house for the least amount of money.

It is something nice you can do for your house, yourself and your family, that you don't have to budget to death. You can brighten up a room, the house, the kitchen, just because you want a change.

Painting is made for the Do-It-Yourselfer. Big changes can be made to your home or apartment's appearance with minimal investment in paint or tools.

Paint is tough. You can scrub painted walls. There are paints that are mildew proof. There are even textured paints that can give your house a whole new appeal.

PAINTS

WHAT'S THE DIFFERENCE BETWEEN OIL BASE & LATEX PAINT?

OIL PAINTS   LATEX PAINTS

OIL PAINTS		LATEX PAINTS
TiO$_2$ Organic Colors Inorganic Colors Extenders	Pigment for Hiding and Color	TiO$_2$ Organic Colors Inorganic Colors Extenders
Mineral Spirits	Thinners for Proper Consistency	Water
Linseed Oil or Soya Oil or Alkyd	Binders for Adhesion and Film Build	100% Acrylic or Vinyl Acrylic or Vinyl Terpolymer

Source: The Rohm and Haas Paint Quality Institute

OIL PAINTS AND LATEX PAINTS both have three key components: pigment, thinners and binders. While similar pigments are used in both kinds of paints, oil and latex use different thinners and binders, as the chart shows.

As the Rohm and Haas diagram indicates, both oil base and Latex Paints have the same three ingredients: Pigments, Solvents or Thinners, and Binders. Pigments give the color. Binders are the "glue" that holds the color to the surface you are painting. They are the key ingredients that give each particular type of paint its distinctive characteristics.

PAINTS

Thinners hold the Pigments and Binders in suspension and allow you to apply them to the surface. When the paint is applied, the Thinner or Solvent evaporates, and the Pigment and Binders oxidize or "cure." This process takes anywhere from a few hours to several days.

The Pigments used in Oil Base and Latex Paints are quite often the same. The Thinners and Binders are different and give the two different paints very different performance characteristics.

In Oil Base Paints, the Linseed or Soya Oil Binders are dissolved in Mineral Spirits. As the Thinner evaporates, the Pigment and Binder form a rigid, water tight film.

In Latex Paints, the chemical Binder (Acrylic, Vinyl Acrylic or Vinyl Terpolymer Polymers) are dispersed, not dissolved, in the water. When the water evaporates the Pigment and Polymer particles pack together and fuse to form a continuous, tough, but not watertight, plastic film.

PAINTS

CHARACTERISTICS OF

OIL BASE vs. LATEX

Oil Base Paints: are far more forgiving. They require less surface preparation, dry slower, and adhere to far dirtier, shinier, or more weathered surfaces. They can also be applied in colder weather. Oil Base Paints are designed to be worked into the surface.

Latex Paints: dry faster, have less odor, are far more tolerant to humidity, far easier to clean up, need only soap and water, and, since they outsell Oil Base Paints better than 10 to 1, there is a greater selection of premixed colors. Latex Paints lay on top of the surface.

PAINTING TECHNIQUE: is very different. With Oil Base Paints you "brush in" and "stretch out" the paint. With Latex Paints you "Ladle it on" and let it "flow off" the brush.

HOW TO CHOOSE WHICH IS BEST FOR YOUR PARTICULAR PROJECT.

The decision as to which paint to use should be made on the basis of surface preparation, humidity, drying time and personal preference.

If you can't do much surface prep, and are going to paint over a rather dirty, shiny or very weathered surface, you have to choose Oil Base Paint. The water in Latex Paint will actually combine with the grime on a dirty surface to form mud. If there's any grease, Latex Paint will not adhere at all.

If the humidity is very high, Latex Paint comes through like a champ. On a high humidity day, Latex Paint will just take longer to dry.

Oil Base Paint, on the other hand, will never dry. You could wind up having to sand, vacuum and wipe down the entire surface with a tack rag, before repainting. In such a case you have to choose a Latex Paint or decide it's too hot to paint and go fishing.

On the other hand, if it's a fine clear day, but rain is immediate, an Oil Base Paint will stand up to the weather. A Latex Paint could actually be washed off by a thunder storm.

When you have already purchased paint that is wrong for present application conditions, you have to make a command decision: Should you rush back to the store and try to exchange your paint...or should you grab a glass of your favorite beverage and watch the baseball game, knowing that this is the best possible use of your time under the present climactic conditions? My chaise lounge was built to help me make decisions like that.

Cold effects Latex Paint to a much greater degree than Oil Base Paints. It effects the property of the paint called "colessing" - the ability of the paint to stay together. In the cold, the chemical combination in Latex weakens and makes it so that the paint will start peeling rapidly.

There are presently some new paints on the market that will let you paint outside in near freezing weather. It is expensive, but well worth the price under certain conditions.

PAINTS

If cold is a problem, ask your retailer's advice on which paint to buy.

If its a nice day, you have a clean, well prepared surface, your choice of paints is one of personal preference. Traditionalists like Oil Base Paint's more "natural" ingredients. They like the thought of the linseed oil "feeding" and protecting the wood. Some even like the meticulous cleaning of their natural bristle brushes in turpentine or paint thinner.

Modernists like the scientific technology of Latex Paints. They like the plastic shield of protection a Latex Paint gives wood. They revel in the easy cleanup, as they just hose down the rollers, then finish up brushes and rollers with a nice soap and water bath.

If all else fails, flip a coin.

One final caution: Remember, that instructions on the paint can are written for ideal conditions: 77° F. temperature and 50% humidity. If it is colder, hotter, dryer, or more humid, manufacturer's instructions will have to be adapted.

I like to talk about windows of opportunity. Good painting conditions include a 55° to 85° F (12.5° - 29° C) temperature window of opportunity. Humidity is more forgiving. The humidity index can be anything from 0% to 80% .

PAINTS

If you are outside these ranges, you may need to select special kinds of paints, or in extreme ranges of heat and cold, rain or complete dryness, may not be able to paint at all.

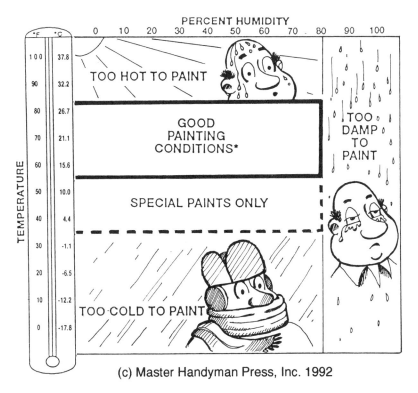

(c) Master Handyman Press, Inc. 1992

*The Ideal Temperature used in making most paint application specifications is 77º F, 50% Humidity. Good Painting Conditions: 55º to 85º F, 0 - 80% Humidity.

TOOLS OF THE TRADE

Chapter II

TOOLS OF THE TRADE

BASIC MINIMUM PAINTING KIT

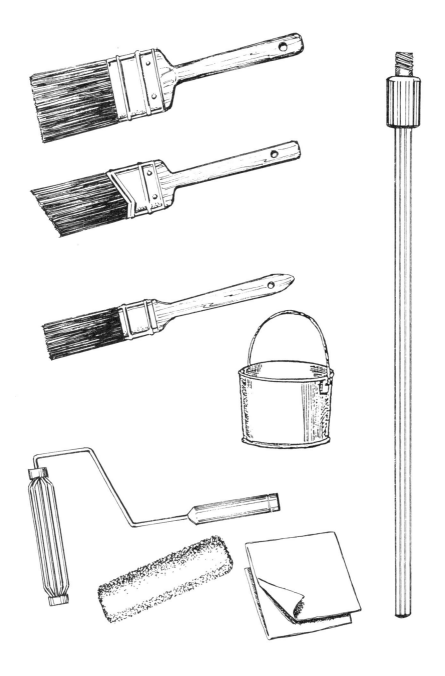

TOOLS OF THE TRADE

The basic minimum you need for painting the inside of a house is a good, professional quality, 2" or 2 1/2" flat brush, an angular cut trim brush, a quality 9" roller, roller pan and an adjustable extension handle. You should also have a 2 1/2 gallon pail, paper and plastic drop cloths and masking tape or Easy Mask(TM).

If you need to paint the outside, just add a 3" or 3 1/2" brush and a proper ladder.

As your needs, challenges and opportunities grow, so will your brush collection. Larger houses and a greater more varied collection of tasks, will cause you to fill out your brush collection over the years.

A COLLECTION OF BRUSHES

Since nine out of ten gallons of paint sold are Latex, my recommended selection of paints is going to be heavily weighted to Latex. Just remember, if you choose to use all Latex Paints, that's fine. But when a particular "opportunity" calls for an Oil Base Primer, go out and buy a brush for the primer.

LATEX BRUSHES

Brushes used for Latex Paint can be made out of nylon, or nylon polyester. Never use a natural bristle brush with Latex Paint. The water in the paint, and the repeated washings will ruin the bristles. Always buy professional quality brushes. The little extra cost, more than pays for itself in ease of use and durability.

TOOLS OF THE TRADE

REMEMBER: NEVER USE THE SAME BRUSH FOR LATEX AND OIL BASE PAINTS. ALSO, NEVER USE THE SAME BRUSH FOR VARNISH AND ANY TYPE OF PIGMENTED PAINT OR STAIN.

INTERIOR BRUSHES

The average homeowner will need three 2" or 2 1/2" brushes. One for Latex, one for Oil , and one for Varnish.

Natural Bristle or high quality Polyester for Varnish.

Natural Bristle or Nylon/Polyester for Oil Base Paint.

Nylon or or Nylon/Polyester for Water Base Paint.

2" OR 2 1/2" BRUSHES

The 2" or 2 1/2" brush is the workhorse of your arsenal. It's an excellent size for many tasks: cutting in, trim work, finishing faces of kitchen cabinets, etc. You'll need three.

TOOLS OF THE TRADE

1   The Varnish brush should be either a very fine natural bristle, a top quality badger hair, or the highest quality polyester.

2   The Oil Base paint brush should be natural china bristle. A good nylon-polyester brush is also all right. Never use a 100% nylon bristle brush with oil paint.

3   The Latex paint brush should be either a good nylon or nylon polyester. Natural bristle brushes should not be used with Latex Paint, because the bristles absorb water, and repeated soap and water washings will gradually dry out the bristles.

Make certain that you mark each brush, so that you do not use the wrong brush. Once a varnish brush has been used with a pigmented coating, it should never be used with a clear coat again.

Interior brushes are cut with a chisel point, so that the paint flows evenly from the bristle.

1" TRIM BRUSH

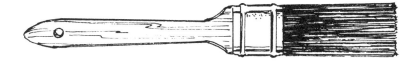

The 1" Trim brush is for all those hard to get at areas.

TOOLS OF THE TRADE

You'll need one for Latex Paint. You may also need one for either oil base or varnish if you do enough work to make it worth while.

If, for some reason, you have to use an Oil Base Stain Kill, for example, and want to use Latex for the final coat, you have to have two brushes. Also remember, that you can use interior brushes for outside work.

RULES TO LIVE BY:

1   CHEAP BRUSHES MEAN CHEAP JOBS.

That doesn't mean you have to sell the family jewels to buy an expensive brush. If you spend $9.00 or $10.00[1] on a good 2" brush, it will never wear out. If you never loan it out, you'll never have to buy another brush.

2   YOUR BRUSH IS ONLY AS GOOD AS ITS LAST
       CLEANING.

If you don't clean your brush thoroughly after each use, it will get old and stiff. You'll have to buy another one.

Clean Oil Base and Varnish brushes in paint thinner or turpentine. Clean Latex brushes with soap and water. Clean and dry thoroughly, then wrap in newspaper, or store in the original container.

---

[1] 1992 US dollars.

TOOLS OF THE TRADE

3   NEVER SOAK YOUR BRUSHES IN A HOT, OR
CHEMICAL BRUSH CLEANER / RESTORER.

The harsh chemicals will ruin the bristles. Train
yourself to thoroughly clean your brushes after each use.

4   NEVER LET YOUR BRUSH STAND ON ITS
        BRISTLES.

Brushes are very carefully designed and crafted to
flow paint onto a surface. Resting the weight of a brush on
its bristles for any period of time, destroys their trim and
shape, destroys the even interior paint flow and ruins the
brush.

Hang the brush by the hole in its handle, even during
cleaning and drying. Store hanging, so that gravity helps
the bristles retain their shape.   The little extra time this takes
is a very worthwhile investment.

TOOLS OF THE TRADE

ROLLERS

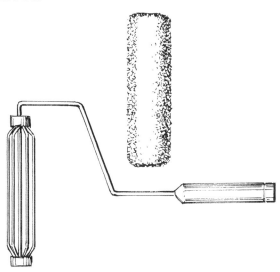

     If reading all about rollers really turns you on, turn to the section on rollers and other painting tools in the Appendix. Otherwise, buy one good 7" or 9", five wire cage roller and forget about it.

     A five wire cage means that five, instead of four, heavy wires support the roller pad. Five wires give your roller pad better support and will keep it round longer. A good one should last for a generation or more.

     Whether you buy a 7" or 9" roller is entirely up to you. It depends on how macho you feel. The 9" roller is the biggest seller by far. But remember, a 9" roller is 30% wider, covers 30% more area, **and is 30% heavier at the end of a long day's painting.**

TOOLS OF THE TRADE

The same thing can be said about roller covers. A $4.50 -- $ 5.00[2] roller cover will give you the proper phenolic core, the proper trimmings and mixture of filaments and the nap you need to get a good paint job.

You may need two covers. One for Latex, one for Oil Base Paints. Also, if your walls have different textures, you may need rollers with different length nap. A smooth wall requires a roller with 3/8" or 1/4" pile or nap. A lightly textured wall requires 1/2" pile. Semi-Rough surfaces call for 3/4" pile. Rough surfaces require 1" pile.

Specific tasks call for specific roller pile thicknesses. We'll recommend the roller you should use, for each specific job in subsequent chapters.

When you change paints, or are painting a different texture surface that requires a different cover, splurge.

The highest quality roller cover is hand sewn lamb skin. If you are a stickler for quality, or plan to do very fine work, go for it. Properly cleaned, a good lambskin roller cover will last and last.

A good nylon-polyester roller, costs half the price and is more than adequate for most tasks.

---

[2] 1992 US Dollars.

TOOLS OF THE TRADE

ROLLER EXTENSION POLE

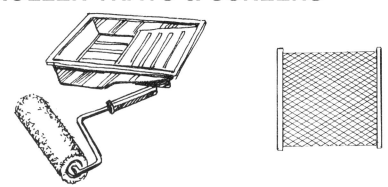

A 4' to 6' wood or metal pole is good. It screws into the roller handle and extends your reach and cuts hours from the job. An expandable pole is even better. It takes up less space and can be adjusted to just the perfect length for the job.

A Roller Extension Pole permits you to stay off the ladder while painting most ceilings and walls. Off the ladder, with both feet solidly planted on the floor, is the safest place to be.

ROLLER TRAYS & SCREENS

A heavy duty, professional model tray gives about 3/4" greater depth than standard or promotional trays. This increase in the amount of your paint supply will greatly decrease the number of trips back to refill your paint supply.

TOOLS OF THE TRADE

An alternative approach is to borrow a trick used by many professional painters. Pour a gallon of paint into the bottom of a 2 1/2 or 5 gallon pail and insert a roller screen. That way you can cover 400 square feet of wall space before you need a refill!

PAINTING MITS

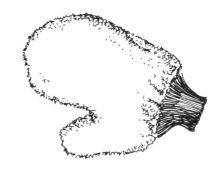

Mits are ideal for painting railings and odd sizes. Watch out for splinters if you use them on deck railings.

PAINT SPRAYERS

Definitely not in the basic painter's kit. Best use inside is in painting furniture. Can do an excellent job painting or staining siding or cinder block. Special additives have to be added to Latex Paint if it is to be used in a paint

TOOLS OF THE TRADE

sprayer. The biggest challenge when spraying is covering too wide an area with too little paint, applying insufficient material to build up the necessary mill finish.

If you are going to rent or buy a paint sprayer, be sure you get a HVLP (High Volume/ Low Pressure) model. An HVLP Sprayer will eliminate the many over-spraying problems and help assure that you apply the necessary mill thickness.

PAINT STICKS

Paint Sticks are hollow roller extension handles which suck up paint, and feed it into the roller. It's a great gimmick for the tool collector who has everything. Some people swear by them. But, it is definitely not part of the basic home owner's kit.

DROP CLOTHS

Drop cloths come in three basic varieties. Plastic, Canvas and Paper. Paper drop cloths are the best for the Do-It-Yourselfer. They protect, but at the same time absorb paint spills. This quality keeps you from slipping or making a mess.

TOOLS OF THE TRADE

If you are careful , you can paint an entire house with two paper drop cloths. Use them four or five times, then throw them away.

Canvas drop cloths are fine for professional painters. They last for years and can be washed. But they are not worth the investment for the casual D-I-Y'er. If you remodel houses for a hobby, that is a different story.

Plastic drop cloths should be used over things too heavy to move, like couches and book cases. Please do not use plastic drop cloths on the floor. They are messy and become so slippery they could put you in the hospital.

A lot of people use bed sheets. Don't. They are too thin. If you're going to use something from around the house, use something thick like old blankets or bed spreads.

STEP LADDERS

Make certain that you get a ladder that will support your weight. Many of the better ladders will have a designated weight load.

Get a 5' aluminum step ladder rated Household Duty # 1 or # 2. A 5' ladder is usually high enough unless you have a cathedral ceiling. A # 1 or #2 grade aluminum ladder will last a lifetime and has enough magnesium in it to be light weight, yet very strong. Budget ladders do not have the performance characteristics you need and can cause a serious injury.

TOOLS OF THE TRADE

If you already have a wooden ladder, make sure you never paint the rungs. Painted rungs can become very slippery and the paint can hide cracks in the wood.

OTHER STUFF

Putty knives, scrappers, sanding blocks, sanding screens, single edged razor blades, caulking guns, are all necessary. They are pretty well self-explanatory. If you need something special, we will explain it in detail when called for in later chapters.

INTERIOR PREP.

Chapter III

INTERIOR PREP.

NOW READ THIS:

Pre-painting preparation takes more time than any other portion of the painting job. About two thirds of the total job time in fact. You can use the wrong paint and still get a good looking job. You can use the wrong brushes, rollers, drop cloths, ladders and still get a good looking job. Bad Prep, on the other hand, always means a bad job.

That makes this one of the most important chapters in the book.

Read it well.

INTERIOR PREP.

What's the best way to get a room ready for painting?

CLEAR FOR ACTION!

Move everything movable out of the room. That includes everything in the closets. I'm serious about the closets. They are an important part of the room. Tacky looking closets make even the nicest paint job look bad.

Everything movable should go into another room for the duration. Large objects, such as book shelves and heavy furniture should be shoved into the center of the room and covered with drop cloths. You may cover these items with plastic tarps or drop cloths, blankets or heavy spreads. No sheets. Sheets will not protect against a heavy spill.

Cover the floor with paper drop cloths, no plastic. Plastic is too slippery. If you have canvas drop cloths or tarps, fine. If there is something in the wall or ceiling, such as a wall mounted air conditioner, or microwave, now is the time to mask it (i.e. protect with paper and masking tape).

Remove shelving, electrical covers, or metal work from the walls. You don't have to mask an electrical outlet plate that you've removed. You don't have to worry about splattering paint on a hot air return that is in the next room. Clean and inspect these items. If they look old and dingy, now might be a good time to replace them.

If anything is stuck fast, not to worry. You can always tape around it. However, it is usually faster to remove than tape.

Next, take the doors down and clean them thoroughly.

Be honest. If you're like most people, doors are the most mistreated part of the house. You know you won't have the patience to do a proper job after the painting is done. Take them down now. Take the hardware off. Inspect the door and fixtures for wear and tear. Oil the handle and lock mechanism.

INTERIOR PREP.

If they are varnished, a thorough cleaning, or a mineral spirit bath might be nice. Then oil all six sides with lemon oil. If more extensive work has to be done on the varnished surface, you'll find instructions later in the book.

If the doors are to be painted, store the doors in another room until you paint the trim.

INSPECTION

Take a look around. Now that the room is completely cleared, are there any signs that the surface is unsound? Is there anything that lets you know that a real problem may lie beneath the surface? Crumbling plaster, cracking, paint scaling, mold?

We don't want to just paint over problems. If you have a problem, determine what it is. Now is the time to fix it. Crumbling or water stained plaster or drywall is a sign that the roof leaks, or you have a plumbing leak somewhere. If you have a water stained ceiling, you may have to go up on the roof and inspect the shingles.

It makes no sense to paint over a problem. It will just reappear. Track the problem down and fix it, **NOW!**

This is a book on painting, so I can't take time to give directions on roof and plumbing repair. After those core areas are fixed, we get to the repair of water damaged plaster, dry wall and wood ceilings and walls. I'll go over these areas lightly, here. They are covered in more detail in my book, *FIX IT FAST & EASY!*.

INTERIOR PREP.

PROJECT: I've got a hole in my plaster or drywall.

TINY NAIL HOLES: Fill with a putty pencil and sand even with the surrounding wall.

SMALL HOLES: Fill with water putty if the area will have to hold weight, or spackling compound if it is just for looks. Sand with Medium Sandpaper.

LARGE HOLES: Make lath out of wood paint sticks or cardboard. Fill with patching plaster. Sand with Medium Sandpaper.

LARGE DRY WALL HOLE: If the area is large enough, saw out a rectangular area of the drywall with a compass saw. Replace with the same size of fresh dry wall and nail it into the studs. Mask the cut areas with dry wall tape. Cover with spackling compound and sand smooth with Medium Sandpaper.

DOOR KNOB HOLE IN WALL: You can fix the hole using the same directions as for "**LARGE HOLES**" above. This is such a common problem that some hardware stores carry pre-made door knob hole patching kits that contain all the materials you need. You can just buy the kit and follow the simple directions.

STRESS CRACKS: Don't patch. Use special expandable wall tapes like Fiba Tape (TM) or Pro Mesh(TM).

INTERIOR PREP.

PROJECT: I've got a problem with wood paneling.

WOOD AND WOOD PANELING REPAIR

SMALL AREA OF ROTTEN WOOD: Gouge out the offending area with a chisel. Fill with a stainable, Latex Wood Putty. Sand with Fine Sandpaper.

LARGE AREA OF ROTTEN WOOD: Cut out the offending area and replace. You may want to make the patch slightly smaller than the rotten wood. Then fill the empty area with wood putty and sand with Fine Sandpaper.

WATER STAINED WOOD OR PANELING: No problem. You will just paint the entire wall with an Oil Base Stain Kill. More complete directions are found in the painting chapters.

WATER RUINED PANELING: Sorry, if the paneling is beginning to separate because of the water, no repair is possible. Replace with a matching piece of paneling.

INTERIOR PREP.

PROJECT: What's the best way to clean the surface for painting?

Washing the walls and ceiling before painting is the most important step of the entire painting process. You have to get rid of all the oils, grease and dust before you paint. Different rooms call for different concentrations of cleaner.

IMPORTANT: Never use a petroleum distillate based cleaner before painting. I don't care what the commercials say. A petroleum based cleaner will leave a slight oil trace on the surface. This oil trace will stop the paint from adhering properly and make you a very unhappy camper.

INTERIOR PREP.

WALL AND CEILING WASHING TECHNIQUE:

I prefer using long handled sponge mops and staying off the ladder. You may decide you want to use a hand-held sponge and climb a ladder. The hand-held sponge method lets you apply more liquid, and keeps you "close to the action." It is also a lot more work.

To do the job right, you need two 2 1/2 gallon buckets, 2 sponges or sponge mops, 2 pair of rubber gloves, 2 pair of goggles.

Wall washing is a great two person job. The first person washes the area. The second person, lets the cleaning solution stay on the wall at least two minutes, then rinses. The reason for the two minute delay, is to let the cleaning chemicals do the work. This is especially important in dirty or greasy areas like kitchens and baths.

Sorry, but you want to be a little messy here. Use a lot of cleaning solution, and a lot of rinse water. This will definitely mean that you have to have your paper drop cloths on the floor. If you have to wash around wallpaper, protect the wallpaper with paper drop cloths, or paper sheeting, attached with specialized masking tape which will not tear the wallpaper.

Goggles and gloves are a must. Tri-sodium Phosphate (TSP) and skin were never made to keep company. Protect your hands with the rubber gloves. Fold the gloves over into a cuff at the top so that the water doesn't run down your arm. Wear goggles to protect your eyes from splatters.

INTERIOR PREP.

KITCHEN AND BATH:

Wash down with a 2 oz. dry measure solution of TSP and water. In a standard 2 1/2 gallon pail, you will add 4 oz. of TSP to 2 gallons of water.

If the walls are especially greasy, use Dirtex (R), or add 2 oz. of household Ammonia.

Rinse especially thoroughly in the kitchen. Change your water about every half a wall. Change water about three times when doing a standard ceiling.

If the kitchen has a fan, remove the blades and wash them thoroughly. The edges are prone to get greasy.

FAMILY ROOMS OR OTHER ROOMS WITH WOOD BURNING FIREPLACES:

Use the same directions as for kitchens, above. Fireplaces are wonderful, but usually permit at least a little smoke to escape and leave creosote traces on the wall and ceiling surfaces.

FAMILY ROOMS AND HALLS IN HOMES WITH NICE HEALTHY(READ MESSY) KIDS:

Sorry, but little kids and teenagers mean oily, sweaty, dirty hands on the walls. Better use the 4 oz. (dry measure) TSP solution.

INTERIOR PREP.

BEDROOMS, LIVING ROOMS, HALLS & FAMILY ROOMS WITHOUT KIDS.

Wash with a 2 oz. (dry measure) TSP solution. A quick rinse and you're ready to paint.

ALL ROOMS IN HOUSE WITH A SMOKER:

Ugh! Tobacco tar is hard on walls, but at least you can get rid of the residue with a 4 oz. TSP solution. Imagine what it is doing to the family's lungs. You can't use TSP there.

WOOD PANELED WALLS:

4 oz. TSP solution. Rinse very thoroughly.

CEMENT BLOCK WALLS:

4 oz. TSP solution. Rinse. You will need at least a 48 hour drying time before painting.

INTERIOR BRICK & STUCCO:

4 oz. TSP solution. Rinse and let dry 48 hours.

INTERIOR PREP.

INTERIOR PREP.

PROJECT: I need to remove the wallpaper before I paint?

STRIPPABLE WALLPAPER REMOVAL:

Just loosen a corner and pull. If it's really Strippable wallpaper, and was applied correctly, a big tug will pull it down in great big sheets.

PROJECT: My removable wallpaper isn't going quietly. What do I do?

CONDITION: Tightly bound to wall surface.

MATERIALS NEEDED: Liquid Wallpaper Remover, 4 oz. TSP solution.

SPECIAL EQUIPMENT NEEDED: Paper Tiger(TM); Electric Wallpaper Steamer, Squeegee with a 4 to 6 foot Extension Handle.

TIME REQUIRED: 1 day.

PROCEDURE:

1   This is a messy job. Make certain that you have drop cloths on the floor. This is one case where you may want to use some plastic drop cloths on the floor, right next to the wall on which you are working. You will wind up scraping the wallpaper "gunk" onto the drop cloths and transferring it directly into plastic trash bags.

INTERIOR PREP.

2   Score the wallpaper with the Paper Tiger(TM). This penetrates the wallpaper with a series of little holes which will let the water or steam penetrate behind the wallpaper.

3   Take a sponge and a pail full of luke warm water and wet down a small test section of the wall thoroughly .

4   Wait a few minutes.

5   Scrape the wall paper off the surface with a large putty knife. Be careful not to gouge the surface.

6   If the test section was successful, continue throughout the room. If not, you may want to rent an Electric Wallpaper Steamer.

7   Wash surface with a 4 oz. TSP solution. Change rinse water constantly.

8   Once the wall has been cleaned and dried, feel the surface with your bare hand. If it feels smooth, fine. Proceed with your painting project.

9   If the wall feels "ricey", you will have to wash it down with Liquid Wallpaper Remover.

10   Squeegee the gunk off the wall with a Squeegee and a 4 to 6 foot Extension Handle.

11   Re-wash with a 4 oz. TSP solution. Rinse constantly.

INTERIOR PREP.

PROJECT: It still isn't coming down.

CONDITION: Wallpaper is tightly bonded to the wall surface.

MATERIALS NEEDED: Liquid Wallpaper Remover, TSP.

SPECIAL EQUIPMENT NEEDED: Paper Tiger, Electric Wallpaper Steamer, Squeegee with 4 to 6 foot extension handle.

TIME REQUIRED: 1/2 day.

PROCEDURE:

This is a great two person job. If you can recruit the extra pair of hands, one person steams, the other scrapes. Wow! Who says we don't know how to have fun.

1   Score wallpaper with the Paper Tiger(TM).

2   Fill the Steam Wallpaper Remover with water, plug it in and start steaming the wallpaper off at one corner of the room.

3   Carefully scrape away the loosened wallpaper with a putty knife.

4   If wallpaper does not come off easily, you need to re-steam the area.

INTERIOR PREP.

5   If the surface feels quite "ricey" to the touch after you have scraped off the wallpaper, wash it down with Liquid Wallpaper Remover.

6   Squeegee the gunk off the wall.

7   Wash down with a 4 oz. TSP solution. Change rinse water constantly. This is another great two person job!

PROJECT: I need to remove non-strippable wallpaper from my wall prior to painting.

CONDITION: Wallpaper is on tight, except at a couple of corners. There is a little bit of mildew showing on one wall.

Use the same directions as we listed for the problem strippable wallpaper, above. Add two cups of Chlorine Bleach to the TSP solution you use to wash the wall with mildew. Make a note to add a mildewcide to the paint on that wall.

PAINTING TECHNIQUES

Chapter IV

PAINTING TECHNIQUES

CHOOSE YOUR WEAPONS:

Many "How To" hobbyists have an entire arsenal of power painting equipment. I don't. You may choose to use a spray gun or power roller. If that makes the job fun, go for it.

Most professional painters stick with brushes and rollers for the majority of their painting tasks. This is not because they want to do their work slowly. It is because they tend to get superior results and maximum speed with the traditional equipment. They keep special equipment for special needs.

SPRAY EQUIPMENT:

If you choose to paint your rooms with spray equipment, here are a few tips:

1	Do the ceiling first. Paint the width of the room, starting from the window side.

2	Paint in 2 foot wide strips.

3	Over lap slightly.

4	Three light coats are better than one heavy coat.

5	When painting walls, start at the top of the wall and do 2 foot wide vertical strips.

6	Wait until all other paint is perfectly dry and can be masked before you start the trim.

PAINTING TECHNIQUES

7   Don't spray paint windows.

NOW, FOR THE REST OF US:

I use a brush / roller combination technique. I find it the fastest way to get the best results.

1   Make certain that the entire room is cleaned, prepped and sanded.

This includes window troughs. Dirt and dust are the painter's biggest enemies.

2   Make certain that all windows are free moving.

If the double hung windows have been painted over many times, you can probably work them free by a combination of pounding the frames with the palm of your hand and cutting through the dry paint between the sash and the joint with a utility knife.

If that still doesn't work, try cutting and separating the sash from the frame with a wide putty knife. If necessary, you can gently pound the putty knife handle with a hammer. Work all the way around both the inside and the outside of the window.

If that doesn't do it, there are special window paint cutting tools at the hardware store for this job.

Worst case scenario: Make certain that the window is completely free around both the inside and the outside, then gently pry the window up or down from the outside.

PAINTING TECHNIQUES

3   Decide upon your schedule of attack.

In the days when Oil Base Enamel was king, painters usually painted: trim, windows, ceiling, walls. One of the primary reasons for this was that painting the trim gave off few fumes, so the painter was clear headed for the most meticulous work. Painting the walls put the most fumes in the air and came last.

Now that Latex is most often used and fumes are not a problem, the order of priority is often: ceiling, walls, windows, trim. The window frames and trim are often an eggshell or semi-gloss enamel.

For the purpose of this chapter, we are going to go: ceiling, walls, windows, trim.

Mixing and Transporting Paint:

Make certain that your paint is properly mixed. Have the paint mixed at the store. Before you start to paint empty the paint can into a 2 1/2 or 5 gallon mixing bucket. Make certain that all the bottom sediment goes into the bucket, then mix thoroughly.

If you are going to need several cans of paint, box the paint. That is, little by little, pour all the paint into one large 5 gallon bucket. Mix the complete batch of paint together. Then pour all but the first half gallon back into the paint cans. Seal the cans.

Never use the can the paint was transported in when you are painting. This can was made to transport and store paint. It is a very messy container for painting.

PAINTING TECHNIQUES

When you paint, use a rimless can or pail. A half gallon pail or kettle is perfect for brush work. A 2 1/2 to 5 gallon bucket with a roller grill insert is good for high speed roller work. You may also choose to use a roller tray.

Brush Work:

Always use the right brush. Natural bristle is best for Oil Base Paints. Nylon or Nylon Polyester is best for Latex. Natural bristle is best for clear varnish.

Condition the brush. If you are using Oil Base or Alkyd, dip the brush in mineral spirits or turpentine before you start to paint. If you are using Latex, dip the brush in water.

A brush has only two purposes: 1, to transport the paint from the container to the surface; 2, to spread the paint on the surface.

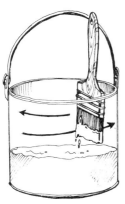

To get the proper amount of paint in the brush, dip it straight down into the paint about one third the bristle length. Then draw the brush straight up and out of the paint.

Tap the sides of the inside of the paint pail with the width of the brush, to release excess paint.

Do not pull the sides of the brush over the top of the container. This only runs the risk of cutting the bristles and usually drains too much paint from

PAINTING TECHNIQUES

the brush.

Ceilings:

Painting is a great togetherness project. If you do it together, one person should do the brush work. The other person should handle the roller. I actually prefer to paint alone. I do the initial brush work first. Then, the roller work.

Before you start painting the ceiling, you may want to cheat a little and skip to the section on painting windows. Most windows have to be painted in two separate sections. If you do the first part now, the initial window paint can be drying all the time you do the ceiling and walls.

INITIAL BRUSH WORK:

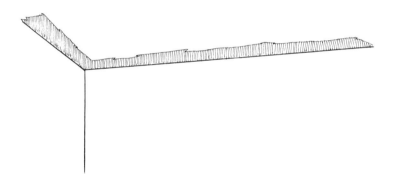

The first job when painting the ceiling is to paint a three to four inch wide border around the ceiling with a 2" trim brush. Start near a corner and paint a small, thin line next to the wall. Then broaden out for the rest of the border.

PAINTING TECHNIQUES

Be sure to paint right up to the wall edge with your initial stroke. You will use this to guide you when you paint the wall border.

When your brush starts to feel empty, pull away gently (feather) and refill the brush. Bring the refilled brush next to, but not touching the end of your previous paint stroke. Complete your first application stroke away from the freshly painted area. Then, on your return stroke, brush into the previously painted area. Feather at the end of the stroke. This will form a more uniform job.

ROLLER WORK:

Always paint across the width of the ceiling, not the length. Start on the window side of the room and paint inward. Divide the width of the room in your mind's eye into 3' X 3" or 4' X 4' sections.

Paint the first section in the corner on a window side. Then paint the second section beside the first, extending another four foot along the width of the room.

PAINTING TECHNIQUES

There is no reason to use a ladder unless you have a very high ceiling. Attach an extension handle to the roller (brush attachments are also available). Use a medium nap roller cover for most paints. Paint a big "W" on the ceiling in the first section pushing the roller away from you. The first stroke should be about 2" away from the ceiling border you just painted. Roll slowly so that you do not splatter paint.

After you have made the first "W", repeat with another "W". This second "W" pattern should overlap the first and go into the ceiling borders. Repeat with a third and forth "W" pattern until the 4' X 4' block is filled evenly.

For your second 4' section, refill your roller and repeat the 4 "W" s. Repeat this process until you have painted the complete width of the room. Then, begin the process all over again, until you have worked you way across the entire width and length of the room.

Walls:

I start walls, the same way I do ceilings. Do the initial brush work first, then the roller work. Finally, it's back to the brush for the windows and trim.

INITIAL BRUSH WORK:

Completely frame all the walls with a 3" to 4" border. Use a 2" trim brush. If the ceiling and the walls are different colors, wait until the ceiling is dry. Then, very carefully draw a bead of paint parallel with, but not quite touching, the ceiling.

PAINTING TECHNIQUES

     If the walls and ceilings are the same color cut in 3" to 4" borders. Paint the border along the ceiling first. Then do the sides and lower molding.

ROLLERS:

     In your mind's eye, divide the wall into 3' X 3' or 4' X 4' blocks. Begin at the top of the ceiling and work your way across the wall.

     Start with a "W" pattern close to, but not touching the ceiling and wall borders you have just painted. Right handed people are usually more comfortable painting left to right. "Lefties" usually start on the far right and work their way left. Roll slow enough to prevent splatters.

     Fill in with a second "W" pattern that goes into the borders. Continue with a third and fourth "W" pattern to fill the block evenly.

PAINTING TECHNIQUES

Work your way completely across the wall, then start a second strip across the wall. Always start the initial "W" with a full roller. Finish up with the gradually drying roller. Make certain that you do not cover too much area with too little paint. If you find that you are stretching the paint too far, reduce the size of the section. Do not reload your roller in the middle of a section, or you run the risk of having an uneven paint job.

If you decide that you want to brush, instead of roll, this part of the project, use a 3" to 4" brush. Paint 3' deep rows across the wall.

WINDOWS:

Windows vary greatly. Some have metal or vinyl frames that should not be painted. Others are made of wood, or trimmed with wood that should be painted.

Use a 1 1/2 or 2" sash brush to paint window sashes.

There are basically three different kinds of windows: Casement, Sliders, and Double Hung. Each should be painted a little bit differently.

PAINTING TECHNIQUES

Casement Windows:

When painting Casement windows, paint the edges first. Let dry completely, then paint the frames.

Sliders:

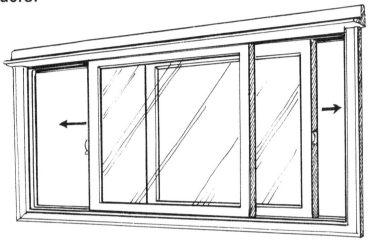

When painting Sliders, slide the inner, right hand window to the left and the left hand window to the right. Paint the edges and exposed frame sections. Let dry completely, then slide back to the closed position and finish painting the window.

PAINTING TECHNIQUES

Double Hung Windows:

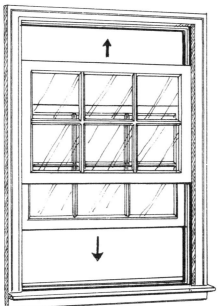

Painting Double Hung windows is simple if you do it right. Remove all hardware, then push the upper sash all the way down to about 4" above the sill. Pull the lower sash up to about 4" below the upper window frame.

1   Paint the (usually hidden) inside lower frame of the upper sash.   Do not paint the bottom edge of the lower frame, because this will be seen from the outside.

2   Paint the window trench, the bottom slot into which the lower sash slides.

3   Let dry.

PAINTING TECHNIQUES

4   Push the upper and lower sashes to within 3" or th...
usual positions. Complete painting the window.

5   Finish painting the upper sash.

6   Paint the entire lower sash.

7   Paint the horizontal Mullions.

8   Paint the vertical Mullions.

9   Paint the Frame.

10   Paint the Stool and Apron.

11   Let dry thoroughly. Then push to closed position.

If you are giving the windows and trim two coats, you will have to go through this entire procedure twice. Wait until you have painted the second coat to scrape away the paint you accidentally painted on the window.

About a week after the windows have been painted, lower the upper sash and raise the lower sash completely, to make certain that they are easy sliding.

Trim:

Make certain that the wall is completely dry before you start painting the trim. You may want to use masking tape on the wall around the floor molding and door trim.

Don't worry if the trim has many different angles. A good trim brush can get paint to all of them rapidly. Apply

PAINTING TECHNIQUES

the paint with one long, fast stroke. Feather the end of the stroke so that each section fades into the other evenly. Then, come back, fill in and smooth the section with shorter strokes.

The trim work is often the shiny accent to the room. Make certain each section is perfect before you begin the next.

When you have finished one section of trim, start the next section about a half inch from the end of the prior section. Fill in and feather in on your return stroke to provide a uniform coating.

You may want to use a metal triangular paint shield to protect the floor or carpeting when you paint the bottom of the floor molding.

Brush & Roller Maintenance:

Be sure to protect your brushes, rollers and paint trays or buckets when you take a break, stop for the day or finish painting.

When you take a break, you can wrap your brushes and rollers in aluminum foil. This will usually also work for overnight storage.

Paint trays and buckets can be covered with aluminum foil during a short break. However, paint should be returned to its storage container and sealed over night. The paint tray and/or bucket should be cleaned out each night so that dry paint does not begin to adulterate the next day's fresh paint.

PAINTING TECHNIQUES

When the job is finished, brushes and rollers must be cleaned thoroughly. The first step is to work all loose paint out of them with a brush comb. The curved upper side of a brush comb does a great job on roller.

CLEANING BRUSHES USED WITH WATER BASED PAINT:

Then, if your paint was a water base, rinse thoroughly with warm running water. After flooding the brush, work soap into the bristles and clean the brush thoroughly. Start at the ferrule (the metal strip that holds the bristles to the brush), and work your way down. Once the brush is completely dry, hang from a nail until it is completely dry, then wrap in brown paper and store on its side.

CLEANING ROLLER COVERS USED WITH WATER BASED PAINT:

If you need to clean a roller that has been used with water base paint, rinse thoroughly with warm water, then work liquid soap into the nap and suds, then rinse the remaining soap away. Once it is clean, work the excess water out with your hand and stand on an angle to dry.

Once dry, wrap in brown paper. Store upright, never let the roller rest on its nap.

CLEANING BRUSHES USED WITH OIL OR ALCOHOL BASED PAINTS:

You need to wear rubber gloves when removing oil or alcohol based paints from brushes and rollers.

PAINTING TECHNIQUES

Work the brush in jars of mineral spirits, turpentine or other solvent solution. Once the solvent turns milky, start using fresh solvent solution in another jar.

If you can not get all the paint out of the brush, drill a hole in the handle and suspend the brush in solvent over night. Always hang the brush. Never, let it stand on its bristles.

When the brush is completely clean, work the excess solvent out of the bristles and hang the brush on a nail until it is dry. Then wrap in brown paper and store on its side, or hang it bristles pointing down.

CLEANING ROLLER COVERS USED WITH OIL OR ALCOHOL BASED PAINT:

Soak the roller in solvent in a clean roller tray. Put on your rubber gloves and work the solvent through the nap of the roller. Change solvent whenever it gets cloudy. Dirty solvent can be strained and reused for cleaning again and again.

When the roller is completely clean, work the excess solvent out of the roller with your gloved hands, then stand the roller upright to dry.

To make certain that drainage from the drying roller does not injure the surface it is standing on, stand the roller on cloth or newspaper, on top of oil cloth or other water proof material.

When dry, wrap in brown paper and store upright.

CLOSETS & DOORS

Chapter V

CLOSETS & DOORS

CLOSETS

In most cases you will be using the same paint that you are using on the rest of the room. The primary reason for this tip is to remind you that closets are rooms in and of themselves.

Don't paint the closet as an after thought if you have a little left over paint. The closet should be painted first. When you measure it to see how much paint you need for the closet, add about 25%. The closet is such a small room, it is inefficient. It will take more paint than a normal room. Be sure to include the ceiling.

PROJECT: I need to paint my clothes closet. It hasn't been painted for 20 years.

CONDITION: Old, dirty, paint worn away in places.

MATERIALS NEEDED: TSP, your choice of Oil Base or Latex Water Base interior paint.

SPECIAL EQUIPMENT NEEDED: None.

TIME REQUIRED: 2 Days.

PROCEDURE:

1   Wash down closet walls and ceiling with a 2% solution of TSP. Rinse well.

CLOSETS & DOORS

2 Let dry 4 hours. If necessary, put a fan in the room so that it dries properly.

3 Apply 2 coats of paint.

4 Let dry one day between coats.

Doors

IMPORTANT INSTRUCTIONS FOR ALL NEW DOORS:

Hang the door first.

Make certain that it is sized perfectly <u>before</u> you paint.

Remove the hardware and finish the door.

This is the only way that the vital edges of the door will have the protection they need.

CLOSETS & DOORS

Remember: All doors have six sides.

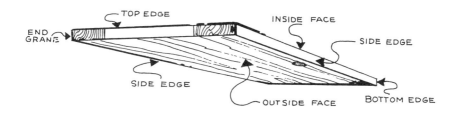

PROJECT: I want to stain a new, hollow core, interior door.

CONDITION: New.

MATERIALS NEEDED: 120 or 150 Grit Garnet Sandpaper, Tack Rag, 100% Cotton Rag, Stain of your choice.

SPECIAL EQUIPMENT NEEDED: Saw Horses.

TIME REQUIRED: 1/2 Day.

CLOSETS & DOORS

PROCEDURE:

1   Put door on saw horses. Rub hand over surface and sand any rough spots smooth.

2   Vacuum.

3   Wipe any stray specks off with a Tack Rag.

4   Using a 100 % cotton rag, wipe on your choice of Oil Base or Water Base Interior Stains. Once the door has attained the desired color, wipe off excess stain with another 100% cotton rag.

5   Four big "if"s.

        If an Oil Base Stained Wood Door gets too dark, wash it off with mineral spirits before the stain dries. This will lighten the stain.

        If a Latex Water Base Stain was used, you can wash it off with water.

        If the stain has dried before you decide that it is too dark, you are going to have to treat the door with a stain remover, and give it a wood bleach bath before restaining.

        If the stain is too light, celebrate. Just add another coat of a slightly darker stain. Wipe off the excess. Be very careful not to make the new coat too dark.

CLOSETS & DOORS

PROJECT: I want to varnish a new, pine, interior door.

CONDITION: New.

MATERIALS NEEDED: 120 or 150 Garnet Sandpaper, Tack Rag, 100 % Cotton Rag, Wood Conditioner,Soft Wood Sealer or Pre-Stain Sealer, Stain if desired, Danish or Antique Oil Finish.

SPECIAL EQUIPMENT NEEDED: Saw Horses, Sponge Brush.

TIME REQUIRED: 1 1/2 Days.

PROCEDURE:

Remember: all doors have six sides. It is very important for you to finish all sides. Pay particular attention to the end grain. Be sure to let your door acclimatize itself to its surroundings. Your home has a different temperature and humidity level than the store or lumber yard. Let your door set for at least two days before you do anything to it. Do not stain, varnish or paint on a high humidity day.

1   Put the door on saw horses and lightly sand away any rough spots with the 120 or 150 grit garnet finishing sandpaper. Your door has already been pre-finished by the manufacturer. That was on a production line. Run your bare hand across the surface and sand away any rough spots.

CLOSETS & DOORS

2   Apply a soft wood sealer, pre-stain sealer or wood conditioner with a sponge brush or pad applicator.

3   If you want to change the color of the wood, stain it now. Apply stain with a 100 % cotton rag. Wipe off the surplus stain with another clean 100 % cotton rag.

4   Let dry overnight.

5   Apply the varnish finish coat. I prefer one of the wipe-down Danish Oil or Antique Oil finish systems. They give a richer sheen and are much easier to apply.

SETS & DOORS

PROJECT: I want to paint a new, hollow core, interior door.

CONDITION: New.

MATERIALS NEEDED: 120 or 150 Grit Garnet Sandpaper, Tack Rag, plus your choice of a Premium Oil Base or Latex Water Base Satin or Egg Shell Interior House Paint, or Semi Gloss Interior Trim Paint.

SPECIAL EQUIPMENT NEEDED: Saw Horses.

TIME REQUIRED: 1 1/2 Days.

PROCEDURE:

1   Put door on saw horses and run your hand over the surface. Smooth out any rough spots with the sandpaper.

2   Vacuum.

3   Wipe any stray specks off with a tack rag.

4   Paint all six sides of the door with your choice of paints. You can roll Latex Paints, but I prefer working in Oil Base Paints with a natural bristle brush.

The wood is going to just "drink in" this first coat. Make certain that you use at least the recommended amount of paint.

CLOSETS & DOORS

Remember, the end grain on the bottom and top edges of the door is where almost all of the door's problems start. Make certain that you do an extra good job covering the end grain on the doors edges.

Wait until the first coat is completely dry before applying the second coat.

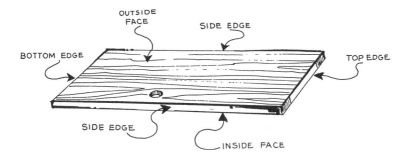

OUTSIDE FACE
SIDE EDGE
BOTTOM EDGE
TOP EDGE
SIDE EDGE
INSIDE FACE

CLOSETS & DOORS

PROJECT: A varnished door was painted with Latex Paint. Now the paint is peeling. I want to solve the problem and repaint.

CONDITION: Peeling paint.

MATERIALS NEEDED: 50 and 100 Grit Sandpaper, Texture Off(TM), Denatured Alcohol, Oil Base Stain Kill, Oil Base Semi Gloss Interior Paint.

SPECIAL EQUIPMENT NEEDED: Nothing.

TIME REQUIRED: 1 1/2 Days.

PROCEDURE:

1   Apply a liberal coat of Texture Off(TM). This is a unique product designed to remove Latex Paint. Follow directions on can. If paint does not scrape off, it was not Latex Water Base Paint.   Use a paint and stain remover to remove Oil Based Paints.

2   Wipe door down with Denatured Alcohol.

3   Apply an Oil Base Stain Kill.

4   Let dry 3 - 4 Hours.

5   Apply 2 coats of an Oil Base Semi Gloss Paint.

CLOSETS & DOORS

PROJECT: I want to paint a formerly varnished interior door.

CONDITION: Good, but old, and knocked up a bit at the bottom where people accidentally hit it with their feet, the vacuum cleaner, etc.

MATERIALS NEEDED: 50 and 100 Grit Garnet Sandpaper, Wood Filler, Liquid Sandpaper, Tack Rag, Oil Base Stain Kill, Oil Base Semi Gloss Paint.

SPECIAL EQUIPMENT NEEDED: Saw Horses.

TIME REQUIRED: 1 Day.

PROCEDURE:

1   Put the door on saw horses. Take off all the hardware. Rough up the surface with the 50 Grit Sandpaper, then sand smooth with the 100 Grit.

2   Vacuum and

3   Wipe with a Tack Rag.

4   Apply Liquid Sandpaper to all 6 Edges of the door.

5   Let Dry.

6   Apply one coat of Oil Base Stain Kill.

7   Let dry 4 hours.

CLOSETS & DOORS

8   Apply 2 coats of a good, Oil Base Semi Gloss Interior Trim Paint. Be sure to let the first coat dry over night, before applying the second coat. Do not paint on a muggy day.

PROJECT: I've got a beautiful oak, interior door. It's been painted many times. I want to take off all the paint and refinish it, bringing it back to its original stained and varnished beauty.

CONDITION: Door in good condition, but many layers of old chipped, hard gloss, Oil Base Paint.

MATERIALS NEEDED: Slow Acting 3M or Dumond Chemical Paint Stripper, Wood Bleach, 120 Grit Garnet Sandpaper, Tack Rag, Wood Conditioner, Soft Wood Sealer or Pre-Stain Sealer, Stain if desired, Danish or Antique Oil Finish.

SPECIAL EQUIPMENT NEEDED: Saw Horses, Sponge Brush.

TIME REQUIRED: 3 1/2 Days.

PROCEDURE:

1   Put door on saw horses. Take off all hardware. You will want to replace or shine and recondition hardware when door is finished.

CLOSETS & DOORS

will want to replace or shine and recondition hardware when door is finished.

2   Layer on a slow acting paint remover like Safer Stripper by 3M or Peel-Away by Dumond. Follow directions carefully. Layer on paint remover 1/8" to 1/4" thick, depending upon number of coats of paint. You are better off putting it on too thick, rather than too thin.

3   Leave Paint Remover on for about 24 hours.

4   Peel off the Paint Remover. If areas need to be scrapped off, use steel wool or a plastic spatula. If any Paint Remover remains in ornate trim areas, work it out with rope or string.

5   Wash down with water to neutralize.

6   If discoloration of the wood remains, wash down with Wood Bleach.

7   All this work has raised the grain on the wood. Sand down lightly to make the surface perfectly smooth.

8   Apply a soft wood sealer, pre-stain sealer or wood conditioner with a sponge brush or pad applicator.

9   If you want to change the color of the wood, stain it now. Apply stain with a 100 % cotton rag. Wipe off surplus with another clean 100 % cotton rag..

10   Let dry overnight.

11   Apply the varnish finish coat. I prefer one of the wipe-down Danish Oil or Antique Oil finish systems. They give a richer sheen and are much easier to apply.

CLOSETS & DOORS

PROJECT: My louvered closet doors are at least thirty years old. They have been painted a dozen times. I want to remove all the paint, bring back the natural finish, stain and varnish them.

CONDITION: Worn, paint chipped, etc.

MATERIALS NEEDED: Heavy Bodied, Methaline Chloride Paint & Varnish Remover, Denatured Alcohol, 0000 Steel Wool, Wood Bleach, 100 Grit Sandpaper, Tack Rag, Safe & Simple Stain(TM), VOC a Varnish.

SPECIAL EQUIPMENT NEEDED: None.

TIME REQUIRED: 2-3 days.

PROCEDURE:

1   Spread on a heavy bodied Methaline Chloride Paint and Varnish Remover like you were icing a cake. Do not brush, just glop it on.

2   Follow the directions on the can for the waiting period. The more coats of paint, the longer you have to wait.

3   Scrape off the paint carefully with broad putty knife. If you are not getting all the paint off, let the remover work for a little while longer before you scrape it away.

CLOSETS & DOORS

4   Wash off the door with and a bucket of Denatured Alcohol and 0000 Steel Wool .

5   If stain remains, bleach the entire door with wood bleach.

6   The bleach will have raised the wood on the door. Lightly sand with 100 Grit Garnet Sandpaper.

7   Vacuum.

8   Wipe down the entire door with a Tack Rag to get rid of any dust particles.

9   Apply a coat of Safe & Simple Stain(TM). This formulation is very user friendly. Wipe on with a rag, then wipe off, when the wood has reached the desired color.

10   Let dry at least 4 hours.

11   Apply 4 coats of a VOC Varnish. Use a polyester bristle brush.

CLOSETS & DOORS

INTERIOR PAINTS: WHERE TO USE WHAT

Finish	Uses	Comments
FLAT PAINTS	General use on walls and ceilings.	Hide surface imperfections; stain removal can be difficult. Use for uniform, non-reflecting appearance. Best suited for low-traffic areas.
EGGSHELL OR LOW LUSTER PAINTS	Use in place of flat paints on wall surfaces, especially in halls, bathrooms and playrooms. Use on trim in place of semigloss paints for a less shiny appearance.	Resist stains better than flat paints and give a more lustrous appearance.
 **SEMI-GLOSS PAINTS**	Kitchen and bathroom walls, hallways, children's rooms and playrooms, doors, woodwork and trim.	More stain-resistant than flat paints and easier to clean. Better than flat paints for high-traffic areas.
HIGH-GLOSS PAINTS	Banisters and railings, trim, kitchen cabinets, bathroom and kitchen walls, furniture, door jambs and window sills.	More durable, stain-resistant and easier to wash. But the higher the gloss, the more surface imperfections will be accented.

Source: The Rohm and Haas Paint Quality Institute

96

KITCHENS & BATHS

Chapter VI

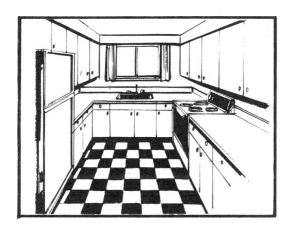

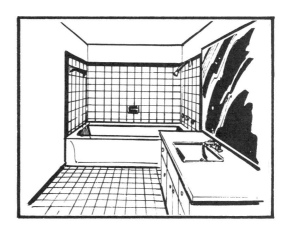

KITCHENS & BATHS

PROJECT: I want to lighten my stained, kitchen cabinets.

CONDITION: Cabinets are in good condition.

MATERIALS NEEDED: Wood Bleach, Light Stain (if desired),Crystal Clear VOC Varnish.

SPECIAL EQUIPMENT NEEDED: Refinishers Gloves, Goggles, Synthetic Steel Wool(TM) by 3M, Tack Rag, Vacuum

TIME REQUIRED: 1 week.

IMPORTANT: If you use VOC Varnish do not use regular steel wool. If even one little strand is embedded in the wood, it will run and look very obvious.

PROCEDURE:

1   Take off all the doors and do separately.

2   Take the hardware off the doors.

3   Remove stain and varnish with a good stain and varnish remover. If you use one of the non-toxic slow acting removers, you can apply the remover to all of the cabinets. Then, wait a day, and scrape it all off.

4   Sand with a fine sanding screen or fine sandpaper.

5   Swab on wood bleach. Wait 3 or 4 minutes, then wipe down with a rag lightly dampened with water. The

KITCHENS & BATHS

water stops the bleaching action.

6   Let dry 3 - 4 hours.

7   Sand and stain if desired. Dip 100% cotton rag into stain, ring out. Rub onto wood.

8   Apply 2 coats of VOC varnish.

9   Lightly rub down with 0000 Synthetic Steel Wool, or 400 grit garnet Sandpaper, vacuum, then tack rag.

10   Apply 2 more coats of VOC varnish.

WARNING: Do not try to cook food while you are doing this. Smoke, grease, any impurities can ruin the job.

KITCHENS & BATHS

PROJECT: I'm bored with my Kitchen Cabinets. I want to change their color and pickle them.

CONDITION: Good Condition.

MATERIALS NEEDED: Paint & Varnish Remover, Synthetic Steel Wool(TM) by 3M, Pickling Solution, VOC Varnish.

SPECIAL EQUIPMENT NEEDED: None.

TIME REQUIRED: 2 1/2 to 4 days.
PROCEDURE:

Make sure you are very good friends with a neighbor, or plan on eating out a lot. Your kitchen is going to be completely out of action for 3 or 4 days.

1   Take doors off of cabinets and remove all hardware.

2   Remove the entire original finish. Air pollution is a real problem in the kitchen. I recommend opening the windows and using a slow acting, environmentally friendly paint and varnish remover, such as 3M Safest Stripper(TM) or Safe & Easy (TM) by Dumond Chemical.

Apply very liberally. Dab on like frosting a cake. Use a cheap, throw away nylon or nylon polyester brush for this. Do not try to use a foam brush. It will disintegrate while you are working.

KITCHENS & BATHS

These removers are very good but slow acting. You will probably be able to apply a liberal coating to all your kitchen cabinets, before beginning the scraping process.

Remember each door has six sides. You have to do all of them.

Scrape off finish . Use a wood or plastic spatula so that you will not accidentally gouge the finish.

3   If the paint and/or varnish is not completely removed, repeat as often as necessary.

4   Wash down the raw surface with mineral spirits or denatured alcohol.

5   All these chemicals will have raised the grain of the wood. Smooth down the surface with Fine Sandpaper.

6   Vacuum or dust.

7   Rub entire surface with a tack rag to remove any dust that's left.

8   Apply Pickling Solution with a 100% cotton rag or a sponge. Deft(TM), Minwax(TM) and many others make them ready to use.

9   Let dry one day.

10   Apply a minimum of 3 coats of VOC Varnish. VOC Varnish is the proper choice for this because it is completely clear and will never yellow.

KITCHENS & BATHS

Each coat of varnish will dry completely within one hour. So you can do multiple coats in a single afternoon. If the surface needs to be smoothed out, lightly sand between the second and third coats only. Vacuum and tack rag.

PROJECT: I want to strip and pickle my doors and door frames.

CONDITION: Good condition, but old chipped paint.

MATERIALS NEEDED: Paint Stripper, Denatured Alcohol, 3M Synthetic Steel Wool(TM), Alcohol Based Stain Kill, Pickling Solution, VOC Varnish.

SPECIAL EQUIPMENT NEEDED: None.

TIME REQUIRED: 2 1/2 Days

PROCEDURE:

Same instructions as for stripping and pickling kitchen cabinets, above. However, you are dealing with rather large expanses of different woods. Your door may be oak or birch. The frames are probably pine. Different woods have different absorption qualities. They have to become uniform before pickling solution is applied.

KITCHENS & BATHS

Wash down the surface with denatured alcohol and smooth the surface with Synthetic Steel Wool(TM), before making the decision. If paint is still in the joints and pores of the wood, try this:

1   Paint entire surface with an alcohol based stain kill. This stain kill melts into the paint and gets into the pores of the wood.

2   Re-strip the surface with heavy bodied Paint Stripper.

3   Smooth out the grain with 0000 steel wool.

4   Wash down surface with denatured alcohol.

5   Return to pickling instructions, starting with step # 6.

KITCHENS & BATHS

PROJECT: I want to repaint my kitchen cabinets.

CONDITION: In good condition. Painted with enamel that is now showing wear from constant cleaning. Normal amount of kitchen grease.

MATERIALS NEEDED: TSP, Oil Base Stain Kill, Oil Base Interior Semi Gloss or High Gloss Enamel Paint.

SPECIAL EQUIPMENT NEEDED: 2 1/2"China Bristle or Badger Bristle Paint Brush.

TIME REQUIRED: 3 to 4 days

PROCEDURE:

1   Take cabinet doors off cabinets and remove all hardware.

2   Clean thoroughly, inside and out with a 4 oz. dry measure TSP solution.

3   Rinse thoroughly.

4   Dry overnight. Next morning give the job a touch test. The feel of the cabinet surface should be dry and slightly rough. There should be no feeling of grease and no chalky dust.

If you feel grease, you did not wash thoroughly. The cabinets have to be re-washed. If you feel and see chalky dust particles, you did not rinse thoroughly. The cabinets have to be re-rinsed.

5   Paint cabinets and doors with an Oil Base Stain Kill. This step encapsulates any grease and stains you have not been able to remove from the cabinets.

6   Let dry 4 hours or more.

7   Cover with 2 coats of a premium quality Oil Base Enamel. Make certain that you are not doing this on a muggy day. Dry thoroughly, at least over night, between coats. Let second coat dry at least one day.

This would be a good time for the family to go on a three or four day vacation or camping trip. The longer your paint job has to cure before you put the doors back, and fill the cabinets with dishes, the stronger it will be. Extra curing time, translates into a better, longer lasting, more beautiful job.

KITCHENS & BATHS

PROJECT: I have glossy varnished Kitchen Cabinets. I want to repaint.

CONDITION: Good condition, but old, yellowed and worn looking.

MATERIALS NEEDED: 80 Grit Garnet Sandpaper, Liquid Sandpaper, Oil Base Stain Kill, Oil Base Semi Gloss Enamel.

SPECIAL EQUIPMENT NEEDED: 2" - 2 1/2" China Bristle, or Badger Hair Bristle Brush.

TIME REQUIRED: 2 1/2 Days.

PROCEDURE:

1   Your biggest problem when painting a glossy surface is to provide a good surface for the new paint. Start by taking off all doors, removing all hardware and powder sanding all shellacked surfaces.

Powder sanding is just using a medium sandpaper to cut the shellac sufficiently to form a light powder over the entire surface.

2   Vacuum.

3   Wash down entire surface with Liquid Deglosser.

4   Cover with Oil Base Stain Kill.

5   Dry 4 hours.

6   Apply Oil Base Semi Gloss Paint with China Bristle or Badger Hair Brush.

7   Apply second coat within 24 hours. Waiting longer can ruin the job.

8   Let dry at least 1 1/2 - 2 Days.

PROJECT: I have some birch wood cabinets. They are in good condition, but I want to brighten them up.

CONDITION: Good but dull and dowdy.

MATERIALS NEEDED: Organic Cleaner, Danish Oil Clear.

SPECIAL EQUIPMENT NEEDED: None.

TIME REQUIRED: 2 Days.

PROCEDURE:

1   Deep clean the cabinets with a mixture of 50% water and 50 % organic cleaner.

2   Rinse liberally. The final result should be "squeaky clean" kitchen cabinets.

3   Rub Danish Oil Clear into the wood. You can use a tinted Danish Oil, if you want to do so.

PROJECT: I have a chopping block in the counter by my sink. I need to refinish it in some way that I will protect the wood from the constant water splashes.

CONDITION: Stained and splattered. Needs help, fast.

MATERIALS NEEDED: Organic Cleaner, Chlorine Bleach, 150 Grit Sandpaper, Tack Rag, Mineral Oil.

SPECIAL EQUIPMENT NEEDED: Fan.

TIME REQUIRED: 1 1/2 Days.

PROCEDURE:

1   Make a 5 to 1 water and organic cleaner mixture. Add 1 cup of household Chlorine Bleach. Scrub down the entire block surface. Keep the area moist and let it work for at least 5 minutes.

2   Rinse with lots of clear water. Wipe dry with rags.

3   Bring a fan into the kitchen and run fan overnight.

4   Next morning, check to see if the block surface is totally dry. If it is, sand smooth with 150 grit Sandpaper.

If it is not totally dry, you may have to wait another half or whole day. Do not let anyone use the sink during this time. Do not start sanding until the block is bone dry.

5   Vacuum all dust and tack rag the entire counter area.

6   Apply four coats of Mineral Oil that you buy in drug stores. Pour a small quantity into the palm or your hand like hand lotion. Then rub the oil into the wood with the palm of your hand. The heat of your hand will open up the pores of the wood and allow the oil to penetrate.

Apply one coat every three or four hours. After four coats, you are finished.

7   Let stand for 24 hours before you use the block.

PROJECT: I removed Vinyl Wallpaper with LT-20 and painted. Now, every place I painted is filled with minute Spider Web Cracks. Paint is peeling down to Dry Wall.

The problem is that you did not get down to a sound surface. Saving the day is going to take some doing.

CONDITION: Spider web cracks, Paint Peeling down to dry wall.

MATERIALS NEEDED: TSP, Oil Base Stain Kill, Latex Water Base Interior Satin or Eggshell Paint.

KITCHENS & BATHS

SPECIAL EQUIPMENT NEEDED: Drywall Pole Sander with Sanding Screen.

TIME REQUIRED: 4 Days.

PROCEDURE:

1   Remove all the paint from the surface. The best way to do this is with a pole sander with a Dry Wall sanding screen.

2   Vacuum.

3   Wash with 2 oz. TSP solution. Rinse thoroughly.

4   Let dry overnight.

5   Put on an Oil Base Stain Kill. Let dry overnight.

6   Apply 2 coats of a premium Latex Water Based Interior Satin or Eggshell Wall Paint .

7   Let dry overnight between coats.

PROJECT: The paint on the Green Board in my bathroom is checking. I want to repaint.

CONDITION: Good Condition, but paint checking.

KITCHENS & BATHS

MATERIALS NEEDED: 100 Grit Garnet Sandpaper, TSP, Chlorine, Oil Base Stain Kill, Latex Water Base Satin Paint.

SPECIAL EQUIPMENT NEEDED: None.

TIME REQUIRED: 2 Days.

PROCEDURE:

1   Scrape all the checking paint away from the green board. Sand smooth with 100 Grit Garnet Sandpaper.

2   Wash down with a 2 oz.. TSP solution. If there is any possibility of mold or mildew, add 4 cups of bleach per gallon of water. Rinse copiously.

3   Let dry for 24 hours.

4   When perfectly dry, paint with an Oil Base Stain Kill.

5   Wait 4 Hours.

6   Apply 2 coats of a premium Latex Water Base Satin Paint.

     Shoot to kill if anyone tries to run hot steamy water in the sink or shower during this crucial period.

     Check the label on the paint can for tack time. Make certain that the paint is perfectly dry before applying the second coat.

KITCHENS & BATHS

PROJECT: I want to change the color of all the stained and varnished floor, window and door moldings. I want the new stain to be uniform in color and lighter than present stain.

This is a time consuming back breaking job. The different moldings are made from different woods, from soft pine to hard oak.

CONDITION: Darker than I want and knicked up a little.

MATERIALS NEEDED: Stain and varnish remover, wood bleach, 160 grit Sandpaper, Tack Rag, Safe and Simple or Gel Gloss Stain, VOC TYPE Varnish.

SPECIAL EQUIPMENT NEEDED: Natural Bristle Brush.

TIME REQUIRED: I sincerely hope you have a lot of it.

PROCEDURE:

1   Apply a coat of Stain and Varnish Remover. My suggestion is that you use the slow acting, but very benevolent, Stain Removers like those made by 3M and Dumond Chemicals' Safe and Easy(TM).

KITCHENS & BATHS

They take a long time to work but will lift several layers at a time. They also treat all woods equally. Spread the Stain and Varnish Remover on 1/8" to 1/4" thick depending on the age and number of coats of stain, varnish, etc., that the Remover has to work through. Follow instructions closely.

Wait up to 24 hours before removing. It can usually just be pulled up. Use a wooden spoon or spatula to scrape off any remaining.

2   Wash with wood bleach to remove any remaining color.

3   The Remover and Bleach will have raised the grain of the wood. Sand it down with 120 grit Sandpaper.

4   Vacuum.

5   Wipe the entire area with a Tack Rag.

6   Apply two coats of a product like Safe & Simple(TM) or any VOC Varnish.

7   Let dry a minimum of 4 hours.

KITCHENS & BATHS

PROJECT: My Wet Plaster Bath has many hair line cracks. I want to eliminate the cracks and repaint.

CONDITION: Hundreds of fine cracks, some falling plaster, mold and mildew.

MATERIALS NEEDED: TSP, Chlorine Bleach, Spackling Compound or Patching Plaster, Oil Base Stain Kill, Oil Base or Latex Water Base Enamel Paint, Porter Sept(TM) or Perma White(TM).

SPECIAL EQUIPMENT NEEDED: Pole Sander with Coarse Grit Sanding Screen.

TIME REQUIRED: 2 Days.

PROCEDURE:

If your bath has mold, mildew and steamy windows, it is an indication that there is not enough air in the house. Call in your heating and cooling contractor and have him suggest ways to bring more air into the house. Your, family's and your home's health depends upon it.

IMPORTANT: DO NOT PERMIT SHOWERS IN THE BATH UNTIL ALL WORK IS COMPLETED.

1   Sand the entire cracked area with a coarse grit sanding screen. A screen is used instead of sandpaper because it can be cleaned when it becomes clogged.

KITCHENS & BATHS

Using a pole sander makes the job go a lot faster. You do not have to use a ladder, can cover a larger area in a lot shorter time. The sanding is also a great deal easier because you get the strength of your back and shoulders into the sanding motion, not just your arm.

2   Open the windows and bring in a fan.

3   Wash down the entire room with a 3 oz. TSP and water solution. Wash the mold and mildew area with a 50/50 bleach and water solution. You should use a dual cartridge respirator, goggles and cuffed rubber gloves for this step. Protect your arms and legs by wearing an old long sleeved shirt and pants.

4   Let dry one day.

5   Fill cracks with Spackling compound. If falling plaster has been extensive, use a patching plaster.

6   Sand repaired areas smooth.

7   Vacuum.

8   Paint the entire room with an Oil Base Stain Kill.

9   Let dry a minimum of four hours.

10   Paint with two coats of your choice of an Oil or Latex Water Based Enamel, or Porter Sept(TM) or Perma White(TM) Mildewcidal paints.

If you use Perma White by Wm. Zinser, you do not need the Stain Kill and can eliminate steps 8 & 9.

KITCHENS & BATHS

PROJECT: I want to paint ceramic tile to change the color in the bath.

CONDITION: Tiles are in good condition. Just bored with the color.

ANALYSIS: First thing you have to decide is whether you really want to do this. If you do, there are professional companies that reglaze appliances, bathtubs, sinks, etc. They use different coatings, and will do a far better, stronger job than you can do.

If you are getting a quote on reglazing, call a couple of tile contractors. Replacement may not cost too much more than resurfacing.

Painting with coatings you get at the store will be the least expensive, but the most delicate. Professional resurfacing is far better and stronger, but also, far more expensive. Tile replacement is the best, longest lasting, and most expensive solution.

If you're going to D.I.Y., here's what you need.

MATERIALS NEEDED: TSP, Water Base Stain Kill, Oil Base Enamel Paint.

KITCHENS & BATHS

SPECIAL EQUIPMENT NEEDED: None.

TIME REQUIRED: Extensive, depending on the size of the room.

PROCEDURE:

1   This is a "championship" all time, squeaky clean, cleaning project. Be sure to wear your rubber gloves and goggles. Wash down with a 4 oz. solution of TSP. Really scrub the tile and around the grout lines with a hand brush.

2   Rinse thoroughly, twice. Use huge quantities of water. Maker certain that there is not even the slightest trace of cleaner, soap scum, or any other contaminant. The slightest trace of a contaminant can ruin the job.

3   Let dry at least 4 hours. Overnight is better.

4   Paint with a Water Base Stain Kill, such as 1-2-3 Bin(TM). Do not start the painting process, until you have rechecked every part of the surface and determined that everything is squeaky clean and bone dry.

5   Let dry 4 hours.

KITCHENS & BATHS

6   Paint surface with 2 coats of a premium oil base enamel paint. Best bet is to let dry overnight between coats.

7   Paint job should "cure" at least 2 or 3 days before any warm water or steam is permitted in the room. A week's curing time would be even better.

8   Never clean with an abrasive cleaner. You will ruin the surface. Use Organic Cleaners, such as Clean Away(TM) or a Citrus Cleaner.

WARNING: Keep the kids and pets out of the room from here on out, if possible. A painted ceramic tile surface is very delicate. Just looking at it the wrong way can cause the paint to crack, scratch or peel.

OPPORTUNITY: This is a great opportunity to learn patience and the meaning of unrequited love. Reading poetry is simpler.

OTHER ROOMS
Chapter VII

OTHER ROOMS

PROJECT: I have high gloss Oil Base Enamel walls. I want to change to Latex Water Base Eggshell or Satin Paint in a much different color.

CONDITION: Good but old.

MATERIALS NEEDED: TSP, Satin or Eggshell Latex Water Base Paint.

SPECIAL EQUIPMENT NEEDED: Long Handle for Roller.

TIME REQUIRED: 2 Days.

PROCEDURE:

1   Wash with 2 oz. TSP. Rinse thoroughly.

2   Let dry one day.

3   Roll on one coat of Latex Water Base Stain Kill. Let dry.

4   Now apply your favorite Satin Finish coat.

OTHER ROOMS

PROJECT: I removed Cedar Shingles from a wall. Now, my wall has a combination of adhesive splotches and gouged out dry wall. I want to remove the glue, fill the tears and paint.

CONDITION: Good but old and adhesive is impossible to get off. Dry Wall tears have ruined the surface.

MATERIALS NEEDED: Old Hard Adhesive Remover, TSP, Spackling Compound, Sanding Sponge, Plaster Pencil, Oil Base Stain Kill, Latex Water Base Paint.

SPECIAL EQUIPMENT NEEDED: Roller Extension Handle.

TIME REQUIRED: 4 Days.

PROCEDURE:

1   Pour some Old Hard Adhesive Remover into a jar. Paint to the adhesive with a throw-away brush. Let sit for at least a half an hour. Scrape off with a putty knife.

If some adhesive still remains, repeat.

2   Wash wall with a 3 oz. TSP solution. Rinse thoroughly. Change water often.

OTHER ROOMS

3   Let dry overnight.

4   Fill cracks and gouges with a Vinyl Spackling Compound.

5   Fill the inevitable nail holes, etc., with a Plaster Pencil. Red Devil makes the best Pre-Moistened Plaster Pencil.

6   Apply a coat of Oil Base Stain Kill over the entire wall.

7   Wait 3 to 4 hours.

8   Apply two coats of a Latex Water Base Satin or Flat Paint. Do not use a Semi Gloss.

9   Make sure you wait one day between coats.

OTHER ROOMS

PROJECT: I don't like the Pecan Paneling in my family room. I want to make it look like a regular wall and paint.

CONDITION: Old, stained Pecan Paneling.

MATERIALS NEEDED: Dirtex(TM), Paintable Caulking Compound, Latex Based Stain Kill, CoverAge(R), Heavy Duty Clear Premixed or Metylan Special Vinyl Wallpaper Paste, Oil Based Stain Kill, Latex Water Base Velvet, Eggshell or Satin Paint.

SPECIAL EQUIPMENT NEEDED: Wallpaper Tray, Brush, and Seam Roller.

TIME REQUIRED: 3 days.

PROCEDURE:

1   Clean paneling thoroughly with a 6 ounce per gallon solution of Dirtex(R). Rinse thoroughly.

2   Fill grooves with caulking compound.

3   After caulking compound has set, sand lightly.

4   Paint paneling with a Latex Based Stain Kill.

5   Let dry 4 hours.

OTHER ROOMS

6   Apply CoverAge(R). Cut this special wood chip and fiber wallpaper to size with a pair of scissors. Cut each piece approximately 2" longer than wall height. Brush Vinyl or Heavy Duty Clear Premixed Paste on to CoverAge(R) strips. Let stand for at least 15 minutes. Then hang strips over paneling. Butt strips closely together. Brush excess paste off. Roll the seams with the seam roller.

7   Let dry 24 hours.

8   Apply 2 coats of your choice of a Latex Water Based Flat, Eggshell or Satin Paint. Use a brush along the top and bottom edges and over seams. Then finish painting with a roller, go over seams again.

OTHER ROOMS

PROJECT: I want to brighten the paneling in the bedroom of an older house trailer.

CONDITION: Good condition, but dark from years of oiling with wood preservers.

MATERIALS NEEDED: Mineral Spirits or Paint Thinner, Facial Tissue, Danish Oil Finish.

SPECIAL EQUIPMENT NEEDED: Spray bottle.

TIME REQUIRED: 1 day per wall.

PROCEDURE:

1   Deep clean with mineral spirits or paint thinner. Spray on. Respray as needed to keep area moist for several minutes.

Wipe off with facial tissue. Do not use paper towels. Only facial tissue has sufficient absorbency to get the job done. If necessary, repeat the entire process a second time.

2   Oil with Danish Oil type finish applied with a 100 % cotton rag.

OTHER ROOMS

PROJECT: I want to paint over inexpensive paneling in the bedroom or a house trailer. Actually, painting over photographic plastic laminate or Formica paneling anywhere.

CONDITION: Good condition but has been treated for years with furniture oils and wood preservers.

MATERIALS NEEDED: TSP, Wood Filler, Water Base Stain Kill, Premium Satin Latex Interior Paint.

SPECIAL EQUIPMENT NEEDED: None.

TIME REQUIRED: 2 Day minimum.

PROCEDURE:

1   Clean paneling with a 4 oz. TSP Solution. Rinse thoroughly.

2   Let dry one day.

3   Fill in holes with wood filler.

4   Sand smooth.

5   Vacuum and tack rag.

6   Roll on an Water Base Stain Kill.

7   Let dry a minimum of 4 hours.

8   Roll on 2 coats of a Latex Base Premium Satin or Eggshell Interior Paint.

OPPORTUNITY: This would be a perfect place to try your hand at Faux Painting Techniques. Sponge painting, spattering, rag rolling, or stenciling, can make your walls look like they were wallpapered. Read the Faux Painting chapter in this book.

At the very least, consider painting contrasting color borders. It adds a nice touch of luxury to the room.

Faux painting is quite time consuming. Add one additional day per color for sponge painting, spattering, stenciling or rag rolling. Painting simple borders will add about 1/2 day total to the job.

PROJECT: I want to paint over shiny real wood paneling.

CONDITION: Good. I'm just bored with it.

TIME REQUIRED: 2 days.

PROCEDURE:

Same instructions as for photographic plastic paneling, but use an Oil Base Stain Kill instead of a Water Base Stain Kill.

OTHER ROOMS

PROJECT: I want to remove the wallpaper from the walls and paint the surface.

CONDITION: The wallpaper is old and boring, but on tight.

MATERIALS NEEDED: Liquid wallpaper Remover (possibly), TSP, Onetime(TM) or Perma Last(TM) White crack filler, Oil Base Stain Kill, Velvet, Eggshell or Satin Latex or Oil Base Paint.

SPECIAL EQUIPMENT NEEDED: Paper Tiger, Steam Wallpaper Remover (possibly), Squeegee with 4 to 6 foot extension handle,

TIME REQUIRED: 2 days.

PROCEDURE:

1   Follow instructions for wallpaper removal at the end of Chapter 3.

2   Fill all gouges with Perma Last White or Onetime (TM) crack repair.

3   Sand smooth then vacuum.

5   Cover the entire wall with an Oil Base Stain Kill.

6   Paint with your choice of a Velvet, Eggshell or Satin Latex or Oil Base Paint.

BASEMENTS
Chapter VIII

BASEMENTS

PROJECT: I want to paint the cement floor in the basement.

There are three different answers to this, depending on the age and condition of the basement floor.

CONDITION #1: Preexisting, worn, flaking, painted basement floor.

MATERIALS NEEDED: TSP, Highest Quality (read Expensive) Oil Base Enamel, Mildewcide Additive.

SPECIAL EQUIPMENT NEEDED: Stiff Bristle, Cement Push Broom; Long Handled Squeegee; Extra Wide Roller and Paint Tray; Screw In Extension Handle.

TIME REQUIRED: 6 1/2 Days

PROCEDURE:

This is a summer or fall job. The furnace has to be turned off completely. If you notice paint fumes accumulating, you may have to extinguish gas furnace and water heater pilots. If you have to do this, be sure to turn off gas. When painting has been completed and floor is dry, call the gas company to come and turn the pilot lights back on.

If you have a mildew problem in the basement, buy enough mildew additive at the paint store to add to both coats of paint.

BASEMENTS

WARNING: Be careful about those pilots lights. Make certain to keep ventilation going throughout drying cycle. Open windows before you start.

THIS IS A TEDIOUS JOB THAT CAN NOT BE HURRIED. TAKE YOUR TIME AND DO IT RIGHT.

1   Scrape off all peeling paint.

2   Vacuum thoroughly.

3   Wash down with 4 oz. TSP cleaning solution. If mildew is a problem, add 2 cups of Chlorine Bleach.

BE SURE TO WEAR A DUAL CANISTER RESPIRATOR AND REFINISHER'S GLOVES.

Open all basement windows. Install one or two fans. Keep air circulating during TSP cleaning and rinsing.

4   Rinse thoroughly. Change your rinse water at least every 200 square feet.

5   Dry for at least 48 hours. Keep air circulating with fans. Turn off fans at the end of the drying cycle. You do not want any dust circulating during paint application and drying cycles.

6   Paint first coat of Oil Base Enamel Paint. Add Mildewcide if you have a mildew problem. Oil Base Paint fumes can explode. If you notice fumes getting heavy, turn off pilot lights and gas, don't wait.

BASEMENTS

7   Dry at least 24 hours between coats. Make certain the first coat is bone dry before applying a second coat. If first coat is not thoroughly dry before second coat, your first coat will lift or wrinkle.

8   Apply second coat of paint. Remember to add Mildewcide to the second. coat as well.

9   Let dry at least 48 hours. If you've got the time, let paint cure for an entire week before pushing furniture around.

CONDITION II: Old Dirty, raw basement floor.

MATERIALS NEEDED: TSP, 20° Technical Muriatic Acid Solution, Alcohol Based Stain Kill, Cement Stain.

SPECIAL EQUIPMENT NEEDED: Stiff Bristle Cement Push Broom, Long Handled Squeegee; Extra Wide Roller and Paint Tray; Extension Handle.

TIME REQUIRED: 2 Days.

PROCEDURE: 2 Days.

This is going to seem like a dream compared to the instructions for Condition I.

BASEMENTS

1   Sweep or vacuum very thoroughly.

2   Open all basement windows, use fans.

3   Clean with 4 oz. TSP solution. Use a push broom to spread cleaning solution over the floor. Rinse thoroughly; use plenty of water. Squeegee water into drains.

4   Etch surface with a solution of one part of 20° Muriatic Acid to three parts of water. Scrub on with a deck brush.   When doing this step, wear goggles, boots, long sleeved shirt, old slacks and a dual canister respirator. Read the use and care instructions on page 137 before you begin this step.

5   Rinse thoroughly.

6   Dry overnight.

7   Roll on one coat of cement stain. An extra wide deck roller and tray will make the job a lot easier and faster. Unlike paint, the cement stain leaches into the surface and should not show signs of wear for years. If you have a mildew problem, add a mildewcide additive to the stain.

8   Let dry overnight.

BASEMENTS

CONDITION III: Clean, new basement floor.

MATERIALS NEEDED: 20° Technical Muriatic Acid, Alcohol Based Stain Kill, Cement Stain.

SPECIAL EQUIPMENT NEEDED: Push Broom, Long Handled Squeegee, Extra Wide Roller and Paint Tray; Extension Handle.

TIME REQUIRED: 2 1/2 Days.

PROCEDURE:

1   Sweep or vacuum thoroughly.

2   Open all basement windows, turn on some fans in the basement.

3   Etch surface with one to three solution of Muriatic Acid and water. Scrub on with a deck brush. When doing this step, wear goggles, boots, long sleeved shirt, old slacks and dual canister respirator. Read special Muriatic Acid instructions on page 137 before doing this step.

4   Dry overnight.

5   Roll on one coat of cement stain. Use the extra wide roller and an extension handle.

BASEMENTS

CONDITION IV: New or Used cement slab floor that you expect to carpet or tile in the future.

MATERIALS NEEDED: TSP, Acrylic Cement Water Seal.

SPECIAL EQUIPMENT NEEDED: Push Broom, Extra Wide Roller and Paint Tray, Extension Handle.

TIME REQUIRED: 2 Days.

PROCEDURE:

Never Never paint or stain a cement slab you expect to carpet or tile. Both paint and stain will inhibit the adhesion ability of the glues you will eventually need to use. If you just want to inhibit the dust until carpet or tile is in your budget, apply a good cement sealant.

1   Sweep or vacuum thoroughly.

2   Apply two coats of cement dust stop sealer.

3   Let dry for 24 hours between coats.

WARNING: Do not apply a wood or exterior cement sealer by accident. There is a big difference.

BASEMENTS

PROJECT: I want to remove the tiles from my basement floor and replace with paint.

Don't paint, stain.

CONDITION: Crumbling, lifting floor tiles.

MATERIALS NEEDED: Old Hard Adhesive Remover, 20⁰ Technical Muriatic Acid, Cement Stain.

SPECIAL EQUIPMENT NEEDED: Ice Scraper, Stiff Bristled Push Broom or Deck Brush, Long Handled Roller.

TIME REQUIRED: 1 week.

PROCEDURE:

1   Open up all the windows in the basement. Turn on some fans.

2   Chip off the old tile with a long handled ice scraper.

3   Clean off old adhesive with Old Hard Adhesive Remover.

4   Wash with a 3 to 1 Muriatic Acid 20⁰ Technical Solution (1 part of Acid to 3 parts of water). Scrub on with a deck brush. Read the following instructions carefully before you start:

BASEMENTS

Read the Muriatic Acid label from beginning to end **before** opening the bottle. This is the most dangerous part of the entire project. When doing this step, wear goggles, boots, long sleeved woolen shirt and slacks and a dual canister respirator.

Nylons, polyesters, and other man-made or blended fabrics are worse than useless when it comes to protecting your body from acid.

Make certain that the fans are running, the windows are open, and that children and pets stay well clear of the area during this procedure.

The manufacturer's label suggests that if you get this solution of Muriatic Acid in your eyes, you should flush with water for 15 minutes and see physician immediately. That means that while you flush for fifteen minutes, somebody else calls the doctor, passes on any changes in instructions, gets the car ready, and drives you to the doctor or the hospital (physician's option) immediately.

Please forgive me if I sound like I am treating you like a ten year old. I have a vested interest in you. You are my readers. Your safety and your sight are very important to me.

5   Rinse.

6   Let dry 3 to 4 days.

BASEMENTS

7   Stain with a Latex Water Based Cement Stain. Use a roller with an extension handle.

8   Let dry according to label instructions.

9   The kids and pets can come down now.

PROJECT: I want to paint Poured Cement Basement Walls.

Same Instructions for painting Cement Block Walls.

CONDITION: Good dry condition. If you have damp, crumbling basement walls, the conditions have to be repaired first. Do not paint damp cement, or cement that has leaks.

MATERIALS NEEDED: TSP, Oil Base Cement Paint, or Dry Lok(TM), Perma White(TM) or Latex Basement Cement Wall Paint.

SPECIAL EQUIPMENT NEEDED: Cement Brush, Wire Brush, Cement Paint Brush.

TIME REQUIRED: 2 1/2 Days

BASEMENTS

PROCEDURE:

1   Wire brush and scrape away all loose or cracking cement.

2   Fill all cracks with hydraulic cement.

3   Let dry.

4   Clean thoroughly with a 4 oz. TSP solution.

5   Dry for 24 hours. Run fans all night long.

6   Apply 2 coats of your choice of Latex Basement Cement Wall Paint, Oil Base Cement Paint, or Dry Lok(TM) or Perma White(TM) Paints.

   If you have a good, dry, new basement, Latex Basement Paint is a good choice. If the cement walls tend to be slightly crumbly, or older, Oil Base Cement Paint would be a good choice. If the basement is naturally cool and damp, Dry Lok(TM) and Perma White(TM) are made for those express conditions.

7   Follow label directions, but be sure to wait the recommended time between the two coats of paint. The first coat should be good and dry before you apply the second.

BASEMENTS

PROJECT: I want to repaint my rusted basement window frames.

CONDITION: Rusted and flaking.

MATERIALS NEEDED: Liquid Deglosser, Rust Converter, High Quality Latex House Paint.

SPECIAL EQUIPMENT NEEDED: Wire Brush.

TIME REQUIRED: 2 Days.

PROCEDURE:

1   Scrape and brush off scaly rust.

2   Wash down metal with a Liquid Deglosser.

3   Brush Rust Converter on the rusted parts of the frame.

4   Let dry.

5   Apply two coats of high quality Latex House Paint.

INTERIOR PROBLEMS
Chapter IX

INTERIOR PROBLEMS

PROJECT: I need to paint a surface that has to be washed daily, or very often, like a kitchen or bath area.

The secret to success here is to make certain that the surface is very clean, and adhesion is at the optimum.

CONDITION: Multi-stained kitchen area. Paint has actually been worn away from constant cleaning in some areas.

MATERIALS NEEDED: TSP or Dirtex(R), Oil Base Stain Kill, Oil Base Enamel.

SPECIAL EQUIPMENT NEEDED: China Bristle or Badger Hair Brush recommended.

TIME REQUIRED: 1 1/2 days.

PROCEDURE:

1   Wash with Dirtex(R) or a 3 to 4 oz. solution of TSP.

2   Rinse copiously. Keep changing the rinse water ever ten feet or so.

3   Let dry thoroughly. One day should be enough.

4   Seal up the porosity of the wall with an Oil Base Stain Kill.

5   Let dry 4 hours.

INTERIOR PROBLEMS

6   Apply two coats of a high gloss Oil Base Enamel. Make certain that the first coat of enamel has dried thoroughly before applying the second coat.

Under no conditions should you wait more than 24 hours between the first and second coats of Enamel. If you apply the second coat within this time period the coats of paint will "bond" together. If you wait more than 24 hours, the coats of paint will cure separately and increase the probability of inter-coat peeling.

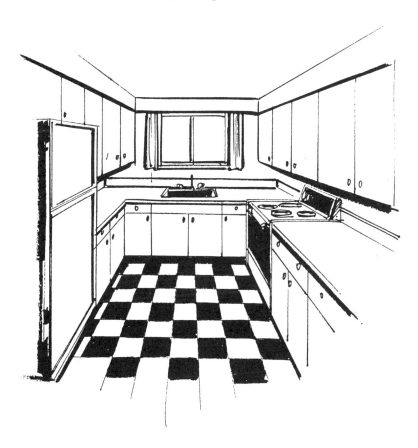

INTERIOR PROBLEMS

PROJECT: I need to paint over Dry Wall that has been damaged by water.

CONDITION: Scaling, water softened Dry Wall.

MATERIALS NEEDED: TSP, Powdered Spackling Compound, Oil Base Stain Kill, Latex Water Based Interior Paint.

SPECIAL EQUIPMENT NEEDED: Sanding Screen with Pole Sander.

TIME REQUIRED:

PROCEDURE:

1   Sand entire area with a Fine Dry Wall Sanding Screen. If the area is large, use a pole sander.

2   Wash entire wall with 2 to 3 oz. TSP solution.

3   Let dry one day.

4   Mix Spackling Powder to thick and heavy cream consistency, and fill in any irregularities where the paint has stopped peeling from the water damage and to even out the Dry Wall.

5   Smooth with Fine Dry Wall Sanding Screen.

6   Prime with an Oil Base Stain Kill.

7   Wait 3 to 4 hours to dry.

8   Finish with your choice of Latex Water Based Interior Paint. You will never make the surface really flat. The greater the irregularities in the wall, the lower the sheen rate recommended for the finish coat. Your best bet is to choose an Eggshell or a Low Luster Finish.

PROJECT: I need to paint over plaster that is falling apart. It had severe water damage but the problem has been fixed.

CONDITION: Scaling, water softened Plaster.

MATERIALS NEEDED: Finishing Plaster, TSP, Oil Base Stain Kill, Flat Latex Interior Paint.

SPECIAL EQUIPMENT NEEDED: Utility Vacuum.

TIME REQUIRED: 2 1/2 - 3 days

PROCEDURE:

1   The first thing you have to do is isolate the loose plaster and find out how deep the loose plaster is. You may have to use plaster screws to tighten up the plaster.

INTERIOR PROBLEMS

In the worst case, you may have to actually cut down the plaster to the brown coat (next to the lathe coat), and build up the plaster to make it uniform again. If this is necessary, you should use a product like Durabond 90(TM), or one of the finishing plasters. This procedure may take two or three applications.

If this area is very large, lets say two walls of a four wall bedroom, you may want to consider dry walling over the plaster. To do this, you would anchor the Dry Wall onto the plaster itself.

If it is a smaller area, or a ceiling, anchor the plaster with Plaster Screws and Washers, and fill with Durabond 90(TM) or a finish plaster.

2   Let dry as recommended on the can.

3   Sand relatively smooth.

4   Vacuum.

5   Wash with a 2 oz. TSP Solution.

6   Let dry one day.

7   Cover with a Oil Base Wall Primer and Sealer over the entire area.

8   Let dry for one day.

9   Apply a Flat Finish Latex or Oil Base Interior Paint.

INTERIOR PROBLEMS

PROJECT: A plaster wall was extended with Dry Wall. I want to make it uniform in appearance and then paint.

Paint alone is not going to do this. You need to use some feathering techniques to build up and feather down. You can plaster a skim coat of plaster over the Dry Wall to bring it up to uniformity.

CONDITION: Uneven.

MATERIALS NEEDED: Dry Wall Tape, Finish Plaster, or Acrylic Texture Paint.

TIME REQUIRED: 1 to 2 days.

PROCEDURE:

1   Finish tape the dry wall.

2   Apply about a 1/8" thick finish plaster to Dry Wall to create a uniform surface with the remaining plaster wall. Some time a scratch(foundation) coat has to be applied before the finish plaster.

ALTERNATE: If this seems like too difficult a project, you may want to look into using ready mixed texture paints, These paints come in three different textures: coarse, medium and smooth.

INTERIOR PROBLEMS

If you want to do this, choose the texture paint that has an acrylic formulation to it. It should even say "Acrylic Texture Paint" on the label. You will get a more flexible film build, and it will be easier to work with and more forgiving as a surface. This is important because the plaster absorbs moisture more readily than the Dry Wall, yet both surfaces have to look the same.

PROJECT: I want to smooth out a textured wall.

The textured surface is most likely a water base paint. If so, you can use a new product on the market called Texture Off(TM) by the Wm. Zinser Co.. This is a ready to use product that comes in a gallon paint can.

Make certain that you use paper drop cloths for this job. Throw them away when you are done.

CONDITION: Textured.

MATERIALS NEEDED: Texture Off(TM), Dirtex(r), Oil Base Stain Kill, Latex Low Sheen Paint.

SPECIAL EQUIPMENT NEEDED: 6" wide Putty Knife, 3/4" Nap Roller, Extension Handle.

TIME REQUIRED: 2 days.

PROCEDURE:

INTERIOR PROBLEMS

1   Roll on a very liberal coat of Texture Off(TM) by the Wm. Zinser Co. Make certain that you cover everything thoroughly.

2   Scrape off the surface with a very broad (6 to 7" Wide) Putty Knife. Scrape the gunk onto the drop cloths.

3   Wash wall with a 3 to 4 oz. Dirtex(R) or TSP Solution.

4   Let dry one day.

5   Apply an Oil Base Stain Kill to establish a uniform porosity to the surface.

6   Let dry 3 to 4 hours.

7   Apply 2 coats of low sheen (Eggshell, Velvet or Satin, etc.) Latex Paints.

Alternate:

If the surface was not treated with a Latex Paint, you will have to sand it smooth. This is an extremely dusty job. If you try it the standard way, with a sanding screen and pole sander, or a sanding wheel, you will have dust throughout the entire house.

There is a new product on the market, made just for the Do-It-Yourselfer, called Sand & Kleen(TM) by Magna. The tool hooks up to a Shop Vac and has a water bath to eliminate dust, but is hard on the arms and shoulders. If at all possible, use the Texture Off (TM).

INTERIOR PROBLEMS

PROJECT: I want to add texture to my wall.

CONDITION: Boring.

MATERIALS NEEDED: TSP, Latex Water Base Textured Paint.

SPECIAL EQUIPMENT NEEDED: Textured Paint Roller with Extension Handle, or Calcimine Brush.

TIME REQUIRED: 1 1/2 days.

PROCEDURE:

1   Wash down walls with a 2 to 4 oz. TSP solution (If this is in a kitchen, or other area, that tends to get greasy, rethink the project. A textured surface acts like a magnet to grease and makes the wall far harder to wash.).

2   Let dry for one day.

3   Apply a Pre Mixed Latex Textured Paint . Use one of the special textured paint rollers. I prefer the yellow, sliced sponge kind, but all the different kinds of Textured Paint Rollers do a good job. One coat and you're done.

If you want, you can create your own textures using a Calcimine brush and Textured Paint.

INTERIOR PROBLEMS

PROJECT: I need to paint over a very rough textured wall.

CONDITION: Good but rough textured.

MATERIALS NEEDED: TSP, Latex Flat Enamel Wall Paint.

SPECIAL EQUIPMENT NEEDED: Garden Sprayer, 1 1/2" Nap Roller with Extension Handle.

TIME REQUIRED: 1 day.

PROCEDURE:

1   Cleaning is the most important part of wall prep before painting. If the texture is very coarse your best bet is to pour a mixture of 2 oz. TSP and a gallon of water into a Garden Sprayer Tank. Spray the cleaner on. Get it good and wet. Change your Sprayer solution to clear water, and spray off the TSP Solution with clear water.

2   Let dry for anywhere between 4 hours and one day depending on the humidity.

3   There are three ways to apply the paint.

   1- You can roll on your choice of paints using a Roller with a 1 1/2" Nap Roller Cover. Use an Extension Handle to extend your reach.

INTERIOR PROBLEMS

2- You can spray on the paint with a light duty Sprayer.

3- You can apply the paint with a Calcimine Brush, being careful to "plop" the paint into all the nooks and crannies.

Your best bet is to use a Flat Latex Water Based Paint. Be warned, you will only get about one half of the coverage specified on the can. So if it specifies 400 square foot coverage, plan on only covering 200 square feet. Make sure you have enough paint in the right color.

If it has been a long time since the last painting, you would do well to use an Oil Base Stain Kill to seal the porosity of the surface before the cover coats. This will eliminate the shadow effect that often happens when textured walls are repainted. That way you are sure to get some bragging rights out of the job.

INTERIOR PROBLEMS

PROJECT: A room in my house was never finished. The dry wall is hung, taped and one layer of dry wall mud applied. I want to paint the walls now.

CONDITION: Good, but stained slightly.

MATERIALS NEEDED: Dry Wall Mud, Latex Water Base Wall Primer or Latex Water Based Stain Kill.

SPECIAL EQUIPMENT NEEDED: Dry Wall Sanding Screen.

TIME REQUIRED: 1 1/2 Days

PROCEDURE:

1   Put a second layer of dry wall mud over taped area. Make the layer about 7 inches wide so that it overlaps the prior layer on both sides.

2   Let dry.

3   Sand wall smooth with a Dry Wall Sanding Screen.

4   Vacuum.

5   If the wall has been up for less than a year, apply one coat of Latex Wall Primer. If the wall has been up for more than one year, apply a coat of Latex Water Based Stain Kill.

6   Let dry four hours.

7   Apply two coats of Latex Interior Wall Paint.

PROJECT: I need to paint over very sticky paint. It never really dried properly. Probably there was a greasy or dirty surface.

CONDITION: Sticky.

MATERIALS NEEDED: Dry Wall Sanding Screen Medium to Coarse, Liquid Deglosser, or Heavy Bodied Paint and Varnish Remover, Denatured Alcohol, Liquid Sandpaper, Oil Base Stain Kill, Finish Paint of your choice.

SPECIAL EQUIPMENT NEEDED: None.

TIME REQUIRED: 1 day.

PROCEDURE:

Alternate # 1- Small Area(Window Sill, part of a Bookcase, etc.):

1   Sand the majority of sticky paint away with a Dry Wall Sanding Screen. This will not gum up as rapidly as sandpaper and you can keep cleaning it for maximum efficiency.

2   After you have sanded away the majority of the paint, wash the surface with Liquid Deglosser. Saturate and wipe with a rag. Let dry, then do a little finish sanding as necessary.

Alternate # 2- Large Area (Entire Wall, Door, etc.)

1   Apply a Heavy Bodied Paint & Varnish Remover. Dab it on like you were frosting a cake.

2   Let stand approximately 45 minutes.

3   Scrape off with a large Putty Knife. Be careful not to scratch the surface.

4   Wash off surface with Denatured Alcohol or Liquid Deglosser.

5   Sand smooth with fine to medium screen.

Alternates # 1 & 2:

6   Prime with an Oil Base Stain Kill to seal.

7   Finish with 2 coats of the paint of your choice.

INTERIOR PROBLEMS

PROJECT: I need to paint over peeling paint.

CONDITION: Paint coming off in strips when bumped or washed.

MATERIALS NEEDED: Fine or Medium Dry Wall Sanding Screen, Spackling Compound, TSP, Oil Base Stain Kill.

SPECIAL EQUIPMENT NEEDED: Sanding Screen with Extension Handle.

TIME REQUIRED: 2 days.

PROCEDURE:

1   Remove the peeling paint. Sand down the edges of the area that is not peeled. I suggest you use a medium sanding screen with an extension handle for this job. That way you can get your back and shoulders into the project, rather than trying to do the entire job with your arm muscles.

2   Wash down the entire area.

3   Let dry one day.

4   Fill uneven areas with a spackling compound. Use a spackling compound like Red Devil One Time (TM) or one of the light Permalastics, because they do not shrink.

5   Sand smooth.

6   Cover the entire wall with an Oil Base Stain Kill.

INTERIOR PROBLEMS

7   Wait three to four hours.

8   Apply your choice of Latex top coats.

PROJECT: I am repainting the enameled trim.

CONDITION: Surface is very hard and glossy. Paint will not adhere easily.

MATERIALS NEEDED: Sandpaper, Liquid Sandpaper, Tack Rag, Paint of your choice.

SPECIAL EQUIPMENT NEEDED: None.

TIME REQUIRED: Depends on amount of trim to be painted.

PROCEDURE:

1   Sand the trim lightly. Use 100 grit Sandpaper.

2   Wash down with Liquid Sandpaper.

3   Wipe down with a tack rag.

4   Paint with your choice of Oil Base or Latex Water Base Paints. If you are making a major change in color, use an Oil Based Stain Kill before this step.

INTERIOR PROBLEMS

PROJECT: Many layers of paint has to be removed before repainting trim.

CONDITION: Many coats of old, chipped paint on ornate surface.

MATERIALS NEEDED: Peel-Away #1 System (TM), TSP, Oil Base Stain Kill, Choice of Paint.

SPECIAL EQUIPMENT NEEDED:

TIME REQUIRED: 1 - 2 days.

PROCEDURE:

Dumond Chemical's Peel-Away (TM) is an excellent product, but a great deal of patience is required. Once the product is in place, you have to wait at least one or more days to complete the project.

You can use regular Paint & Varnish Remover, but there will be a lot of fumes. If you use regular Paint & Varnish Remover, try placing 4 mil Visquine on top of the Remover. It will slow down the evaporation of the chemicals and greatly increase the efficiency.

1   If you choose to use Peel-Away(TM), read the label directions carefully. Then spread on a 1/8" thick coat of the Peel-Away(TM) paste on the entire trim surface.

INTERIOR PROBLEMS

2   Cover with the fibrous laminated cloth that comes with the product. It is very important that the entire area be covered.

3   Wait at least 24 hours.

4   Then, just like the name says, "Peel-Away" the entire painted surface coating. The Peel-Away System should remove up to 15 coats of paint. If it is not pulling enough, stop. Let the formulation work for another 24 hours.

5   Rinse with clear water to neutralize the chemical reaction.

6   If necessary, wash with a 2 oz. TSP solution. Rinse.

7   Since you are now down to the bare wood, cover the entire surface with an Oil Base Stain Kill.

8   Apply two coats of your favorite Oil Base or Latex Interior Trim Paint.

INTERIOR PROBLEMS

PROJECT: The paint on my plaster ceiling has blistered. I want to repaint the ceiling and give it a good, easy to clean surface.

The reason for blistering paint on the ceiling is usually wet plaster, due to roof leakage or bad surface preparation the last time the ceiling was painted. Make certain you are not just painting over a problem. Check out the roof for leakage before you paint. If you have a roof leak, fix it first.

CONDITION: Blistered.

MATERIALS NEEDED: Heavy Bodied Paint Stripper, TSP, Oil Base Stain Kill, Latex Enamel Satin or Eggshell Paint.

SPECIAL EQUIPMENT NEEDED: 3/8" Nap Roller Cover.

TIME REQUIRED: 2 days.

PROCEDURE:

There are a couple of alternatives. If the paint is hard, glossy, Oil Base Paint, and/or the plaster decomposition and bubbling covers a broad area, a paint stripper is called for. Use alternative solution # 1. If the spot is relatively small, the plaster decomposition small, and the flaking relatively minor, use alternative solution # 2.

INTERIOR PROBLEMS

The main problem in both cases is alkalinity. The water has carried the alkalinity to the surface. The alkalinity has destroyed the bonding of the paint to the plaster surface. In addition, water was trapped by the paint, pulling on the surface. The extra weight load pulling on the disintegrating plaster, may cause plaster to fall.

Alternative Solution # 1

1   If a small, glossy area of deteriorating paint has to be removed, the best product for the job is a heavy bodied Paint Remover. Follow label direction exactly. Brush Paint Remover on using small strokes like you were icing a cake. Do not hurry this procedure. Follow label directions exactly. Strip all the paint off down to the raw plaster.

2   Wash with a solution of 3 to 4 oz. dry measure of TSP per gallon of hot water.

3   Make necessary plaster repairs. Fill in with water putty or a finishing grade plaster like Durabond 90(TM).

4   Sand repairs smooth.

5   Let dry at least one day. Remember, raw plaster is like a blotter. It absorbs water big time. Make certain that the plaster is thoroughly dry before the next step. All gray color should be gone.

WARNING: If this ceiling is in a kitchen or bath, do not use the room until you have completed all work and it has dried. The same holds true if you have a smoker in the house. No smoking (hopefully forever) in that room until the job is done.

INTERIOR PROBLEMS

6   Cover the entire ceiling with a good Oil Base Stain Kill.

7   Let dry 4 hours.

8   Apply 2 coats of your finish coat. Use a 3/8" nap roller cover.

9   Let dry 8 to 12 hours between coats.

Alternative Solution # 2:

If you just have a large area, try this solution.

1   Use a pole mounted sanding screen to screen away all the bubbling and flaking. Use a Medium screen. Wear goggles and a mask because of the dust.

2   Wash the entire ceiling or wall with a 2 - 3 oz. TSP Solution. Rinse liberally. Change rinse water at least every 100 square feet.

3   Fill in surface with Finishing Grade Plaster.

4   Sand smooth.

5   Rinse off dust.

6   Let dry per instructions.

7   Apply an Oil Base Stain Kill across the entire area.

9   Apply 2 coats of your favorite Latex or Oil Base Interior Paint.

INTERIOR PROBLEMS

PROJECT: I have to paint the new Dry Wall wall and ceiling of a newly enlarged room. The entire room should look the same when the job is completed.

CONDITION: I want to make room uniform

MATERIALS NEEDED: Dry Wall Patch, Latex Wall Primer; Eggshell or Satin Latex Paint.

SPECIAL EQUIPMENT NEEDED:

TIME REQUIRED: 2 days.

PROCEDURE:

1   Blend in new and old surfaces with Dry Wall patch, mud and tape.

2   Sand smooth.

3   Wash entire room with a 2% TSP solution. Damp sponge the new dry wall area. Rinse.

4   Prime the new Dry Wall area with a Latex Wall Primer. This is the only use for this primer.

5   Let dry 8 hours.

6   Paint the entire area with 2 coats of a good Latex Eggshell or Satin Interior Paint.

INTERIOR PROBLEMS

PROJECT: I want to paint the acoustical ceiling tile in my basement.

CONDITION: Old, dusty, stained.

MATERIALS NEEDED: Acoustical Ceiling Tile Latex Flat Wall Paint.

SPECIAL EQUIPMENT NEEDED: Acoustical Tile Roller Cover, Roller with Extension Handle.

TIME REQUIRED: 1 Day.

PROCEDURE:

Acoustic tile was never meant to be painted. However, the following technique will do a great deal to lighten and brighten up the room.

1   Vacuum away as much of the dust and cob webs from the ceiling tile with vacuum cleaner brush and wand attachment.

2   Roll Acoustical Ceiling Tile Paint gently over the tile. Use a very full roller. You do not want to put any pressure on the tile. Let the roller just "kiss" the tile.

4   Wait approximately 4 hours.

5   Roll a second coat of paint over the ceiling.

INTERIOR PROBLEMS

PROJECT: The paint is flaking off the steel frames of my casement windows in the bath. I want to stop the flaking and repaint.

CONDITION: Severe flaking and lack of adhesion on steel frames of casement windows.

MATERIALS NEEDED: Heavy Bodied Paint and Varnish Remover, Denatured Alcohol, Oil Base Stain Kill, Paint of Choice.

SPECIAL EQUIPMENT NEEDED: None.

TIME REQUIRED: 1 1/2 Days.

PROCEDURE:

IMPORTANT: DO NOT PERMIT SHOWERS IN THE BATH UNTIL ALL WORK IS COMPLETED.

1   Brush on Heavy Bodied Paint and Varnish Remover. Do not brush back and forth. Apply Paint & Varnish Remover from one direction only. Lay it on thick, like you were frosting a cake.

2   Let set for 45 minutes.

3   Remove with a wooden spoon or a plastic putty knife.

4   Wash down entire area with denatured alcohol.

INTERIOR PROBLEMS

5   Wipe clean with rags.

6   Use steel wool on rusted areas.

7   Cover rusted areas with Naval Jelly or Oxisolv(TM). The Oxisolv(TM) will take the rust out of any pits that may have formed in the steel.

8   Paint steel frames with an Oil or an Alcohol Based Stain Kill.

9   Let dry for 4 hours.

10   Apply two coats of the oil based paint of your choice. Follow manufacturer's instructions as to drying time between coats.

PROJECT: The old oak trim wood work around my windows has been splattered by Latex Paint. I want to remove the splatters and refinish the trim to bring back the beautiful original oak finish.

CONDITION: Paint splattered Stained Oak Trim, sun bleached around windows.

MATERIALS NEEDED: Goof Off(TM), Sponge Sander - Coarse/Medium, Tack Rag, Wood Sheen(TM) by Minwax.

SPECIAL EQUIPMENT NEEDED: None.

INTERIOR PROBLEMS

TIME REQUIRED: 1 Day.

PROCEDURE:

1   Apply Goof Off(TM) to the Latex Paint. This is a special product just made for Latex Paint removal. If Goof Off(TM) doesn't take it off, it isn't Latex and a paint and varnish remover is needed.

2   Sand all surfaces with a Coarse/Medium Sponge Sander. You do not need to sand down to raw wood. Just sand the entire surface until you raise a light powder.

3   Vacuum.

4   Wipe up any dust traces with a Tack Rag.

5   Apply Wood Sheen(TM) by Minwax with a sponge brush or rag. One or two coats. Apply a third coat if want a darker color.

You must do all surfaces.

INTERIOR PROBLEMS

PROJECT: My brick hearth is severely discolored from a burning soot/creasolte stain. I want to clean it or cover it.

CONDITION: Soot covers a very broad area.

MATERIALS NEEDED: 20° Muriatic Acid, Hearth Sealer or Acrylic Cement Sealer.

SPECIAL EQUIPMENT NEEDED: Goggles, Dual Canister Respirator, Cuffed Rubber Gloves.

TIME REQUIRED: 1 1/2 Days.

PROCEDURE:

The tip below is just solving a symptom, not the core problem. A sooty fireplace is usually a sign of an air starved house. The smoke is being sucked into the home instead of going up the chimney. Consult your heating and cooling contractor about ways to bring more fresh air into the house and solve this problem.

1   Open windows, bring in fans.

2   Put on your goggles, dual canister air respirator, cuffed rubber gloves.

This is a two bucket project. One for Muriatic Acid and Water, the other for Rinse . Read the top of page 137

168

INTERIOR PROBLEMS

before you use Muriatic Acid. Wear goggles, rubber gloves, long sleeved woolen shirt and slacks, and a dual canister respirator.

Pour 6 oz. of Muriatic Acid into a gallon of water. If the 6 oz. solution does not seem to be effective, you man increase the amount of Muriatic Acid to 12 oz..

Use a scrub brush and clean from bottom to top. Wash only a small section at a time. Rinse immediately with plenty of water.

2   Let dry over night.

3   Next morning apply one coat of a Hearth Sealer, or Acrylic Cement Sealer. Make certain that you get in all the cracks and crevices. Use a disposable brush for this job.

PROJECT: I'm taking very old wallpaper off my plaster walls, and the plaster is coming off with the paper. I want to remove the wallpaper and paint a beautiful smooth surface.

We'd have the same solution for this problem whether the wall was plaster or dry wall. The problem is that you got some stuck up wallpaper. This is a personality disorder. Take your wall to see a psychiatrist.

INTERIOR PROBLEMS

Seriously. The problem is not that uncommon. You are a victim of improvements. If you have fifteen or twenty year old wallpaper, nobody knows what adhesive was used. Wallpaper manufacture has changed three times within the past then years. There's no telling what the problem is.

There are some private companies that specialize in removing problem wallpaper. If you want/need to do it yourself, here's my recommendation.

CONDITION: Old wallpaper stuck to plaster, plaster disintegration.

MATERIALS NEEDED: TSP, Spackling Compound, 120 Grit Sandpaper, Oil Base Stain Kill, Satin or Eggshell Latex Water Base Paint.

SPECIAL EQUIPMENT NEEDED: Paper Tiger(TM), 1 Gallon Tank Garden Sprayer.

TIME REQUIRED: 4 Days.

PROCEDURE:

1   Pierce water absorption holes in wallpaper with the Paper Tiger(TM).

2   Mix 10 oz. dry measure of TSP with one gallon of Hot Water.

INTERIOR PROBLEMS

This is a very "hot", chemically active, solution. Take maximum protection. Goggles, Cuffed Rubber Gloves, Dual Canister Respirator. No dogs, no kids, no curious on lookers.

Put solution into a garden sprayer. Spray a 6 foot wide section. Keep moist for 15 minutes. Peel off paper with a putty knife.

I'm very serious about taking the proper precautions. This solution could literally take the skin off your hand. Use a two bucket system to keep the rinse water clear.

3   Rinse with clear water. Use a lot of water.

4   Squeegee off.

5   Rinse again.

6   Squeegee off.

Make certain that the wall does not have any glue traces when you are finished. If there is still some glue, keep rinsing until surface is glue and bump free.

7   Fill any gouges with Spackling Compound.

8   Let dry one day.

9   Apply an Oil Base Stain Kill.

10   Let dry 3 to 4 hours.

11   Apply your favorite Oil Base or Water Base Paint.

INTERIOR PROBLEMS

WOOD FLOORS:

I know I said I wasn't going to talk about finishing floors in this book. If a floor has to be refinished, I recommend that you hire a professional to do it.

However, most floors do not need to be re-finished. If you follow these simple techniques, most of your neighbors will think you refinished your floors, but you'll know different. These are minor, not major techniques. I'll go into them in more detail when I do a book on finishing floors.

Here is the practical, relatively "fast & easy" solution to my most asked floor refinishing question.

PROJECT: I want to brighten my Wood Parquet Floor.

Remember, dust free cleanliness is the key to salvation here.

CONDITION: Good condition, but a little dark and worn from years of waxing, care and wear.

MATERIALS NEEDED: Verathane (TM).

INTERIOR PROBLEMS

SPECIAL EQUIPMENT NEEDED: Sanding Screen Frame mounted on handle, Medium Sanding Screen, 2 1/2" 100% China Bristle Push Chiseled Varnish Brush.

TIME REQUIRED: 2 1/2 days.

PROCEDURE:

1   Clean floor with an Organic Cleaner to get rid of any stray traces of dust, grease, oil, and grime.

2   Let dry thoroughly (overnight).

3   Turn off the blower on your furnace and/or air conditioner.

4   Screen top layer of varnish to a light dust. Use a fine sand paper mounted on a 4 to 5 foot pole. Don't make too much of a job out of this. We are talking about light sanding only.

Remember, you are not trying to remove all the varnish, just getting rid of the accumulated wax and working the top layer of varnish into a fine dust.

Always sand with the grain of the floor boards, never across them. When your sanding screen stops doing a good job, about 1 or 2" from the walls, it's time to get down on your hands and knees and finish the task.

5   Vacuum thoroughly. Any doubts, do it twice.

INTERIOR PROBLEMS

6   Tack rag the entire floor. Pay close attention to your tack rag. If it is getting too dusty, you did not vacuum properly. Repeat step # 5, then re-tack rag.

7   Wait overnight. Do not ever varnish a floor on the same day you vacuumed it. Air borne dust particles can cause disaster.

8   Apply two coats of VOC Polyurethane.

9   Read the Polyurethane can directions thoroughly. The second coat should be applied in strict compliance with time instructions.

FAUX PAINTING

Chapter X

FAUX PAINTING

PROJECT: I want to add some extra flair to my paint job.

Want to add Pizzazz and imagination? Enter the world of Faux Painting. It can turn your walls, doors, mantels, and ceilings into a fantasy land. Faux Painting is a great way to express your creativity. Using these techniques, you are the ultimate authority. By the power of your paint brush, you can make a wall or paneling look like it is marble, wood grained or wallpapered. You get to earn unparalleled "bragging rights."

"Faux Painting" is a sophisticated term for getting spectacular results, using simple tools and techniques. It includes "Sponging," "Combing," "Feather Dusting," 'Rag-rolling," and "Marbling." I'm also including "Wood Graining", "Stenciling", and "Striping" in this section for convenience.

As you can see from the terms, these techniques are usually named after the primary tool used in accomplishing the result. "Sponging" uses sponges. "Combing" uses a comb of sorts. "Feather Dusting", so help me, actually uses a feather duster. Same with "Rag-rolling", "Stenciling", and "Striping".

This section is designed to give you the basic minimum amount of information you need to know to start a wonderful adventure in Faux Painting. But don't stop here. Consult your professional paint store owner or manager. He or she has magnificent four color brochures prepared by major paint companies, like Benjamin Moore Paints and Martin Senour Paints, that will take you every step of the way.

FAUX PAINTING

Your professional paint store will also often offer free Faux Painting classes and demonstrations. You can't beat free, so take advantage of them.

If no classes or brochures are available you've got more than enough information here to begin the adventure. Remember Franklin Delano Roosevelt famous words: "We have nothing to fear but fear itself."

With Faux Painting, there is almost no downside risk. Even if you have a complete disaster, there is no permanent damage. All it takes is another coat of paint. Let's begin!

PROJECT: What's the simplest way to add a dramatic accent?

The simplest way to add a dramatic accent is to add a second dramatically contrasting color. Make the trim stand out. Make one wall a contrasting color. Paint a wall divider a second color and make it really divide.

You can also add a border at the top of the wall, or divide the wall half way between floor and ceiling. This division is often done by installing a chair molding. The lower half, and the chair molding are then usually painted a darker color. The upper half is wallpapered, or painted a lighter color.

FAUX PAINTING

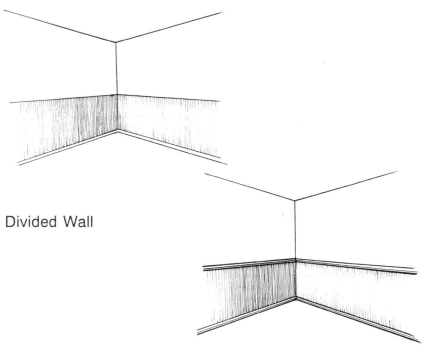

Divided Wall

Wall with Chair Molding.

PROJECT: Divided Wall.

CONDITION: Prepped wall.

MATERIALS NEEDED: 2 different colors of Paint, Masking Tape.

The chair molding is the easier way of doing this because the molding forms a natural divider. However, you can just apply masking tape.

SPECIAL EQUIPMENT NEEDED: Artist's Brush.

TIME REQUIRED: One extra day.

FAUX PAINTING

PROCEDURE: Dividing.

1   Measure half way point. Apply masking tape to the top of the lower half (about 36" from floor) if you do not have a chair molding.

2   Paint from the floor up in your choice of Oil Based or Latex Paints. Use a Brush / Roller combination. If the wall has, or you have installed a chair molding, paint the chair molding the same color.

3   Dry according to can directions.

4   Apply second coat.

5   Let dry completely.

6   Remove masking tape if you do not have a chair molding.

7   Apply masking tape to the border of the newly painted lower half of the wall (use 3M Easy Release Tape).

8   Paint the upper part of the wall with a lighter color.

9   Let dry according to paint directions.

10   Apply second coat of paint to the upper wall.

11   Remove masking tape before completely dry.

12   Let dry thoroughly (at least one full day).

13   Use an artist's brush and straight edge to fill in any areas that are blurred.

FAUX PAINTING

PROJECT: Wall border.

If you want to just add a border to your painted wall, it can take the place of a ceiling molding.

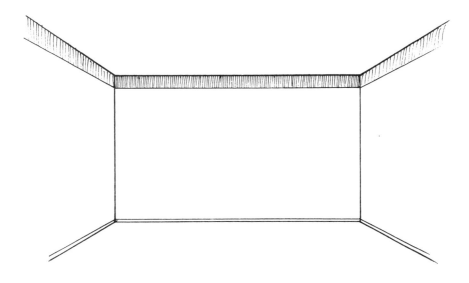

CONDITION: Prepped Wall.

MATERIALS NEEDED: 2 different colored Paints, Masking Tape.

SPECIAL EQUIPMENT NEEDED: Artist's Brush.

TIME REQUIRED: One extra day.

FAUX PAINTING

PROCEDURE:

1   Pencil in a straight line 4 to 6" from the ceiling. This line is the bottom of the border.

2   Create the border by filling in the space between the ceiling and the pencil line with a contrasting or complimentary color to the final wall color. Paint the border with two coats of paint. Use a flat, eggshell or satin Latex Paint.

3   Let dry at least one day.

4   Mask the bottom and top of the border with Masking Tape.

5   Paint the ceiling and walls as you would a regular room with your choice of Latex eggshell or satin paint. Paint two coats.

6   Let dry one day.

7   Remove the masking tape.

8   Use an artist's brush and a straight edge to fill in any irregularities.

FAUX PAINTING

PROJECT: Stencil design to my wall.

Let your imagination soar. You can add a stencil to the top of the wall, or just put in a stencil design treatment in the corners. If you want, you can even add a stencil design to the border you painted in the previous tip. If you decide on this, make one of the stencil colors the same as the primary wall color.

CONDITION: Freshly painted wall.

MATERIALS NEEDED: Clear Acetate or Stencil Pattern,Two or Three Colors of Paint.

SPECIAL EQUIPMENT NEEDED: Artist's Knife, Round Trim Brush.

TIME REQUIRED: One day per color.

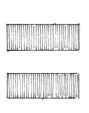

FAUX PAINTING

PROCEDURE:

1   Get a stencil pattern. Most specialty paint or craft stores have sets for sale or you can make your own.

First, create a design. It can be anything. Let's say it's a central 3" star, flanked by a dash on each side, ending with 3" of blank space on either side. The entire design would be about 12" wide and 4" high.

Get four or more strips of clear acetate cut to the exact dimensions of your design. Anchor the design, then trace it on all three of the strips with permanent marker. Put the strips on top of one another to make certain they line up.

Using an artist's knife, cut the center star from one sheet. Cut the two smaller stars from the next sheet. Cut the dashes from the third sheet. Never combine different design elements on the same sheet. Each sheet will utilize a different color paint.

FAUX PAINTING

2   Draw pencil guide lines across the area to be painted. If we used the 4" x 12" example described in step one we would have a top line two to three inches from the ceiling, and a lower line four inches below that.

Lay out the pattern width guide lines. If you see that you are going to get into trouble in a corner, decide upon the solution while you are working in pencil, not paint. You may have to stretch the design out, or "skruntch" it in a little as you get to the corners.

3   Assign the colors to each design element. For the purpose of this example, let's say your big central star is going to be red. Your flanking smaller stars are going to be yellow. Your end dashes are going to be blue. You can choose any paint your want for these design elements. Most designers use Oil Base Enamels because of their strength and brilliance.

4   Apply your first pattern completely around the room. Let's say you start with the big, central star.

PAINTING TECHNIQUE:

a   Pour a very small amount of the dark enamel of your choice in a paint tray or plastic plate.

b   Take a small, I prefer a round, trim brush and dab the tip into the paint, then tap/dab the brush onto the tray or brush until it becomes almost dry.

c   Anchor the stencil to the first wall area with masking tape.

d   Carefully "dab" the trim brush to fill in the central star area.

It is very important that you dab, not stroke the brush, and that you use an almost dry brush (one that has had most of the paint worked out of it). If you do not follow both of these cardinal rules, your paint will run under the edges of your stencil and ruin the job.

e   Work your way completely around the area to be stenciled. Wipe your stencil dry every two or three stencil lengths.
If necessary, cut a second or third stencil.

5   Let dry over night.

6   Next morning, check to make certain that the paint is perfectly dry, then repeat the process with the next design element.

7   Let dry over night.

8   Complete your design with the third design element.

9   Brag!

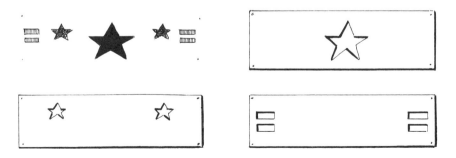

FAUX PAINTING

PROJECT: I want to make my wall look wallpapered.

Ok, bring out the heavy artillery!

I'm going to use this project to explain the basic ground rules, then use different project headings to give details on the various Faux Painting techniques.

To begin with, there are two different major techniques: Positive and Negative. When using the Positive Method, you put on dabs of paint over a base coat. Using the Negative Method you cover a complete wall with a second color, then take off the paint.

The positive technique uses less paint but takes more time. The Negative Technique uses more paint, but usually takes less time.

POSITIVE TECHNIQUES:

SPONGING
RAG ROLLING
FEATHER DUSTING
MARBLING

NEGATIVE TECHNIQUES:

STIPPLING (Reverse sponging)
RAG ROLLING
COMBING OR DRAGGING

FAUX PAINTING

What type of paint should you use?

With the Positive Technique, you usually use Latex Paints and washes for all coats.

With the Negative Technique, even the pros are undecided. Many traditionalists prefer Oil Base or Alkyd Paints because of the greater versatility and slower drying times.

Some paint companies recommend Latex Paints with second, third and fourth colors mixed with water. Some paint companies also make premixed glazes.

No matter what Faux Finish Technique you are going to use, read the following description of sponging. I go into a lot of detail that I won't repeat with other techniques.

IMPORTANT!

Many people do not do Faux Painting because they fear the results will wind up looking like this:

Do not fear. Most books and brochures on Faux Painting use illustrations prepared by top professional painters. They are intimidating to many of us. My wife is a gifted artist. If I had asked her to prepare the examples in

FAUX PAINTING

this book, they would have looked as beautiful as those done by professionals. I didn't want that.

My editorial assistant is a gifted writer and producer. He can work on a dozen projects simultaneously and accomplish them all. But when it comes to anything physical, he is out to lunch. You would never trust him to paint your window trim. He is so bad at "how to" it is literally criminal. I handed him this portion of the book and had him prepare the samples. If you can paint the trim on a window without breaking the glass, ruining the wallpaper, or spilling the paint, you can do better than this. Be fearless. Have fun!

POSITIVE TECHNIQUES:

PROJECT: Sponging

CONDITION: Prepped walls.

MATERIALS NEEDED: 2, 3 or 4 Monochromatic or Complementary Colored Latex Paints, Clear Coat or Glaze Tinted Polyurethane or Latex Acrylic Urethane Finish.

SPECIAL EQUIPMENT NEEDED: Natural Sponges, old 1" Brush.

TIME REQUIRED: 2 to 3 days.

FAUX PAINTING

PROCEDURE:

Deciding upon the final wall coloration is the biggest decision in Faux Painting. You may decide you want the walls to be variations of one color. In this case you would choose different paints from the swatch or chip card at your paint store. Most people want more variation and select different shades of complimentary colors. An example would be a light blue base coat, and perhaps a warm coral and a darker blue sponge coats. These colors would then be muted with a glaze colored Latex Acrylic Urethane.

1   Use a brush and roller combination to paint walls the base coat (light blue in the example).

2   Let dry overnight.

Next morning you begin your sponge coats. You can use one of two techniques. Either decide that you want all the colors to be applied with the same size sponge, or decide you want your first sponge coat to be large sponge size, with succeeding colors applied with successively smaller sponges. No big decision, both make beautiful results.

In any case, you will need to cut a small section off one sponge for use in cutting in the corners of your wall.

Choose the sponges carefully. They will become the design template for your masterpiece.

3   Wet the sponge and wring it out until the sponge is only slightly damp.

FAUX PAINTING

4   Pour a small amount of the first sponge coat paint into a roller tray.

5   Dip sponge into paint and blot excess on tray grid.

6   Practice dabbing the sponge on a practice board or sheet of cardboard. Practice until you really like the sponge designs you are making. Keep working with the practice board with each successive color addition. The practice board becomes your preview of coming attractions.

7   Reload the sponge and start gently dabbing sponge marks about 12" apart until a 4' X 4' area has been covered.

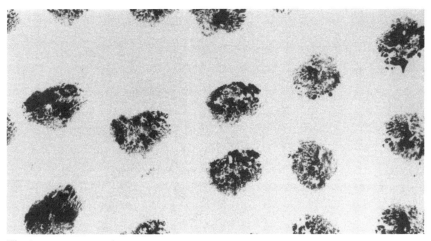

First sponge coat.

8   Go back and fill in the area between the first sponge marks without reloading the sponge with paint. This two step technique assures a constant color across the wall.

FAUX PAINTING

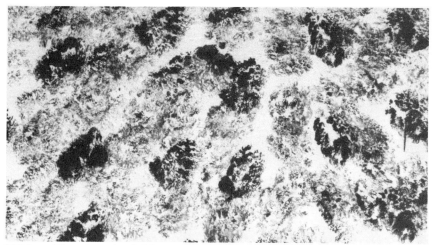

Fill in without replenishing sponge.

The two step 4' X 4' square technique was developed by David Bermann of Scandinavian Decorating Contractors, and appears in Benjamin Moore's *Fantasy Finishes* brochure.

9   Repeat this process until the entire surface you are going to sponge is covered.

10   Remember the small slice of sponge you cut? Cut it so that you have one straight edge.   Dab the sponge into the paint and dab off excess.

FAUX PAINTING

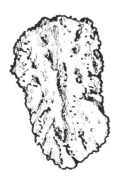

11   Holding the sponge so that the straight edge on the sponge faces the adjacent wall, sponge the corners from top to bottom.

12   Fill in the areas that have been missed by dabbing (not stroking) an old 1" brush in the corners.

13   Make certain the walls are dry to touch before you begin application of the second color. If the wall is at all "tacky" wait two or three more hours.

14   Apply the second sponge color following the same directions used for the first color.

Add second color.

FAUX PAINTING

15   Apply a third color if desired, following the same directions used for the first color.

Highlight with small sponge and third color.

You now have beautiful, but rather fragile walls. It's decision making time again. You can leave the walls just as they are. Most experts recommend applying a clear coat of varnish.

If you love your walls, but would like to tone them down a little bit, make your clear coat a color glaze by adding a pale tint. Benjamin Moore recommends that you use a Latex Acrylic Urethane when making a color glaze. The result adds a touch of subdued mystery. That can't be all bad, right?

16   Wait until walls are dry, then add your clear coat. Coat should be applied with a good brush. A Tapered Nylon / Sable Polyester Blend Brush with Push Chisel Construction is best. Consult with your painting store professional.

FAUX PAINTING

Final glaze coat.

A final word about technique. This is the one time in your life you want your brush strokes to show. Dip brush into a glass jar full of varnish and stroke in on the wall. Go back and cross brush with a herring bone stroke. Accent some of the natural design patterns just for fun.

FAUX PAINTING

PROJECT: Feather Dusting.

PROCEDURE: Same technique as Sponging, only you use the tip of a feather duster instead of a sponge and brush to make the design.

Trust me, when the room is done and decorated, guests are going to start looking at your walls as they would a fine painting. These walls will be a source of pride for years to come.

FAUX PAINTING

PROJECT: Rag Rolling (Positive Method)

CONDITION: Prepped Walls.

MATERIALS NEEDED: Latex Flat, Satin or Eggshell Base Coat, 1 or 2 Complementary Colored Latex Satin Second Coats, Latex Acrylic Urethane Color Wash.

SPECIAL EQUIPMENT NEEDED: Gloves, Rags or RAGROLLER(TM), 1" and 3" Tapered Nylon or Nylon/Polyester Brushes.

TIME REQUIRED: 2 to 3 days.

PROCEDURE:

1   Use a brush/roller combination to cover the walls with the base coat.

2   Let dry overnight.

3   Pour a small amount of your second coat of paint into the paint tray. Dip rag into tray, wring out and twist rag.

FAUX PAINTING

This is one of the times where having kids was really worth the effort. Cotton diapers make perfect rags for wall rolling. If you don't have any diapers, you can use 100% cotton rags or cheese cloth. Cheese cloth actually adds a slight "ridged" line pattern that adds interest to the technique.

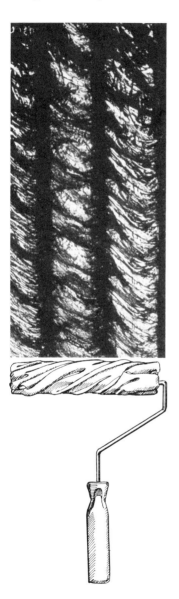

4   Now, starting from the very top of the wall, use your fingers to roll the rag down to the very bottom of the wall.

Boy is this great exercise! The Marine Corps has nothing on you! When you are done with this, your back, knees, arms and fingers are going to be thanking you for this for the next week.

If you want to cheat, try using the RAGROLLER(TM) invented by David Campbell (Today's Practical Products, New Baltimore, MI. (313) 725-4054).

This patented roller tool, invented in 1991, cuts the application time by two thirds and eliminates the aches and pains. It also makes the "rag rolled" design a little more coarse. To me, this slight coarsening is a price I am willing to pay for the time savings and ease of application.

FAUX PAINTING

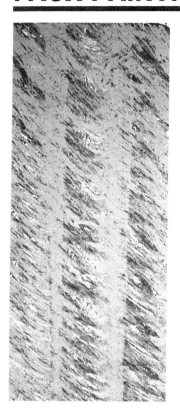

5   Let dry to touch.

6   Apply a second color if desired.

7   Wait until the last rag coat is thoroughly dry, then brush on a finish coat. If you want your design to have more vivid colors, use a clear coat varnish. If you want a more muted look, tint Latex Acrylic Urethane.

Use short brush strokes in multiple directions. Letting brush strokes show adds to the design and improves the finish.

FAUX PAINTING

PROJECT: MARBLING

You could write a complete book on Marbling techniques. I'm just going to go into three different types briefly: Textured Walls and Light Finish Smooth Walls. There are many others.

PROJECT: Textured Walls.

CONDITION: Prepped Textured Wall, or just washed, newly Texture Painted Wall.

MATERIALS NEEDED: White Flat Latex Wall Paint, Warm Beige, Gold, Brown, etc. Satin Latex Paint.

SPECIAL EQUIPMENT NEEDED: Texture Roller Cover with Roller and Extension Handle, collection of large and small rectangular Cellulose Sponges.

TIME REQUIRED: 1 1/2 days.

PROCEDURE:

1   Using a brush/roller combination cover walls with a flat white Latex Wall Paint.

2   Mix a wash of one part water with 8 to 10 parts of your second color paint in a pail. Apply the wash to the wall with a large damp sponge. If the result looks splotchy you did it right. This is the one time in your life where you want to have a completely covered, but uneven finish.

FAUX PAINTING

3   Now, be creative. Using the edge of the small, rectangular Cellulose Sponge, draw in the marble "veins" in a 4' X 4' section with the second color undiluted paint.

4   Go back and feather out the sides of the veins with a flat, water dampened sponge.

5   Lightly blot the areas between the vein with the broad side of the feathering sponge.

6   Go to next 4' X 4' area and repeat procedure.

7   Complete wall repeating steps 1 - 6.

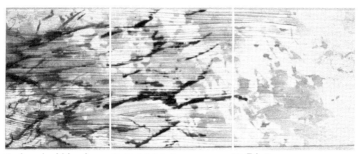

1 Apply Wash.   2 Add Veins.   3 Blot.

FAUX PAINTING

PROJECT: Light Color Smooth Wall Marble.

When marbling, your base color can be any light color you want it to be: white, pale blue, misty green, beige, light yellow. Use the same base tint in the Color Wash that completes the project.

CONDITION: Prepped Wall.

MATERIALS NEEDED: Light or White Latex Flat Wall Paint, Light Gray Latex Glaze, Dark Gray Latex Paint, color tinted Latex Acrylic Urethane.

SPECIAL EQUIPMENT NEEDED: Newspaper, 100% Cotton Cloths, Artist's Brush, old 3" Brush.

TIME REQUIRED: 2 days.

PROCEDURE:

If you are doing this for the first time, why not experiment with a 4' X 8' canvas of dry wall just to get the feel of the materials. Remember, you are doing this for fun. Experiment. Try different techniques and textures. If you don't like a test canvas, don't lose heart. Just roll on another base coat and do a new experiment. If you are using a new piece of dry wall for your test, be sure to prime it before applying the base coat.

1   Paint the walls using a brush/roller combination .

FAUX PAINTING

2   Let dry overnight.

3   Pour a small amount of the gray glaze into a roller tray.

4   Crumble up a piece of newspaper, dip it into the glaze and use the newspaper to create "warm spots" on the wall. You will find that these lines will not be even colored or of uniform thickness. Surprise! They are not supposed to be. You are doing it right, Michelangelo!

5   Brush the wall with a dry 3" brush while the paint is still slightly damp. This will soften the lines even more.

6   Working from the "warm steaks" paint in the vein lines. Use the dark gray paint and an artists brush to draw in the lines. Be creative! Put in branching lines, zig-zags, fault lines, wish bones.

        Sometimes your vein line should be in the middle of the gray pattern, sometimes along side of it. Occasionally, you should branch off in an entirely new direction. Hey, this

FAUX PAINTING

is your turn to have fun.

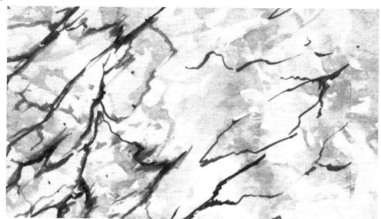

7   Quick, while the artist's lines are still wet, soften the lines by smudging them with a cotton cloth.

8   Dry brush the entire wall.

9   Let dry overnight.

10   Apply the color wash with an old varnish brush.

        This brush will become your official color wash brush because you can never use it again with clear varnish.

11   Oh boy, does this look good. Hug your honey and brag!

        This is just to get you started. You can do many different types of marble. Any color, from jade to rose, to black. You name it. As you grow more experienced, you'll use feathers to trace delicate vein designs. You'll splatter paint on purpose. You'll even start with oil bases and splash water on them. On purpose. Honest!

FAUX PAINTING

Marbling is a great technique for tables, furniture, fireplace mantles and formal stairway trim.

NEGATIVE TECHNIQUES

PROJECT: Stippling (Negative Sponging)

CONDITION: Prepped Wall.

MATERIALS NEEDED: Alkyd or Latex Base Coat (lighter color), Satin Finish Alkyd(oil base) Glaze Coat(s), Mineral Spirits, Polyurethane Clear Coat.

SPECIAL EQUIPMENT NEEDED: Short Nap Roller, 1" & 3" Brushes, Large Natural Sponge, Chamois.

TIME REQUIRED: 1 day plus 1 day per glaze coat.

PROCEDURE:

1   Use brush/roller technique to paint walls with base coat. This coat is usually a lighter color than the glaze coat.

2   Let dry overnight.

IMPORTANT: Steps 3 - 5 have to be accomplished within a ten minute window of opportunity. If you find that you are working slower than this, shrink your work area.

FAUX PAINTING

REMEMBER: Always work from top to bottom.

3   Cover a 3 to 4 foot wide section of the wall with the second color. Cut in the corners and be sure not to leave any brush marks.

4   Who says oil and water don't mix. If it weren't for the water, this Oil Based design wouldn't mix. Dab the glaze with a semi-dampened sponge. Don't be surprised if you don't see a tremendous difference at first. Work from top to bottom. Leave about a 3 inch wide overlap area at the left edge of your work area to eliminate lap lines when you begin the next three to four foot wide work area of the wall.

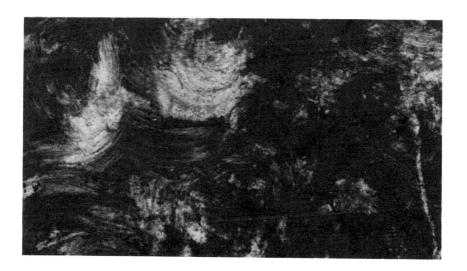

5   Dampen a chamois cloth with water and wring it out until it is only slightly damp. Crumble up the chamois in your hand and begin to dab the entire surface.

FAUX PAINTING

Keep changing the chamois around in your hand so that the pattern varies and so that all the chamois cloth is exposed to the paint. When it is full, rinse it out in a small amount of mineral spirits. Wring out the chamois thoroughly before you go back to work or mineral spirit drips will ruin your job.

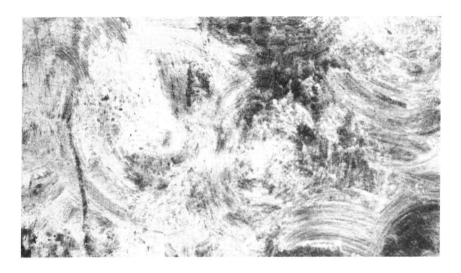

6   Repeat steps 3 through 5 until you have worked your way entirely around the room.

7   Let dry overnight.

8   If you want you may add a second and third glaze coats and repeat steps 5 through 7. Keep in mind, the more glaze coats you add, the more complicated your design becomes and the less the bottom colors will show. One, or at the most, two, glaze coats are plenty for me.

9   Let dry overnight.

FAUX PAINTING

10   When surface is bone dry, cover with a Polyurethane clear coat.

PROJECT: Rag Rolling (Negative Method)

CONDITION: Prepped Wall.

MATERIALS NEEDED: Alkyd or Latex Base Coat (lighter color), Satin Finish Alkyd(oil base) Glaze Coat(s), Mineral Spirits, Clear Coat VOC.

SPECIAL EQUIPMENT NEEDED: 100% Cotton Cloths, RAGROLLER(TM) optional, 1" & 3" Brushes,

TIME REQUIRED: 1 day plus 1 day per glaze color.

PROCEDURE:

1   Apply your base coat. This is usually a lighter coat. However, some people reverse the compliment and make the base coat the darker color. You will get a markedly different effect depending on which you choose. Experiment!

2   Let dry overnight.

3   Apply Glaze coat from ceiling to floor to a 3' to 4' wide section. Use a brush to cut in the corners.

4   Twist a rag tightly. Climb up your ladder and roll the twisted rag straight down to the floor (Oh my aching back).

If you want to reduce the time and work by about two thirds, get a RAGROLLER(TM) made by Todays Practical Products, New Baltimore, MI. (This is a unique product folks. Honest, I do not have stock in the company).

If you use the RAGROLLER(TM) product, it will take you about ten of the replaceable sleeves to do an average size room.

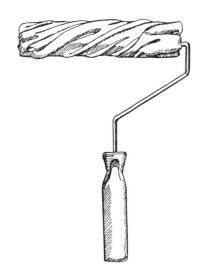

5   Dab in the corners with a wrinkled rag to match.

6   Repeat steps 3 - 5 until room has been completed.

7   Let dry overnight.

8   Repeat with a second color glaze if desired.

9   When the wall is completely dry, cover with a clear coat VOC finish or a tinted Acrylic Urethane Color Wash. The Color Wash gives a more subdued, "smoky" color.

10   Put the furniture back, get cleaned up, and ask your nosiest neighbor over for coffee. Tell him/her/them it didn't take any time at all.

FAUX PAINTING

PROJECT: Combing or Dragging

CONDITION: Prepped Walls.

MATERIALS NEEDED: Acrylic High Gloss Enamel Base Coat and a Glaze Coat.

SPECIAL EQUIPMENT NEEDED: Combing Tool.

TIME REQUIRED: 1 1/2 days.

PROCEDURE:

One of the biggest problems with this technique is that it is too much fun. Once you've mastered the technique, you'll want to do room after room. And each room will look different. Living Rooms and Dining Rooms can be regal. Kitchens can be warm and cozy. Bedrooms can be restful and romantic.

Combing is the fastest and most versatile technique in the Faux Painting Arsenal. The final design depends upon what you use to "comb" the Glaze Coat of paint and the colors you choose.

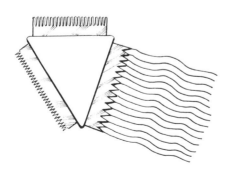 You can use a thick toothed comb and get one design.

FAUX PAINTING

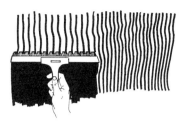

Cut teeth into a window washer's squeegee and you'll get a dramatically different design.

Use a stiff cement brush for your comb and the result will be reminiscent of a formal brocade.

Color combinations can also be wild. Combine pale monochromatic colors and the result will be very restful. Use warm colors and the room will come alive. Use a bright, medium-tone base coat and the result can be electric.

Great color combinations I have seen include: different shades of yellow or blue, mauve and light purple, yellow orange and green, green and black, medium red and gray.

You can also combine straight comb lines with solids, waves, and swirls.

Remember, you do not have to comb all four walls in a room. One combed wall can easily be the dramatic accent for an entire room.

FAUX PAINTING

One person can do this, but it is a better two person job. The person doing the "combing" should have a step stool handy so that they can reach up to the ceiling quickly and easily.

Make sure you have the floor well protected with drop cloths. Paper drop cloths are best, because this gets quite messy and you may want to throw the drop cloths away when you are finished.

1   Use a brush/roller combination to paint your base coat of Oil Base Enamel.

2   Let dry overnight.

3   Mix your glaze coat. No two glaze mixes look exactly alike, so be sure you mix enough to do the entire job. If you are going to use a formal Alkyd Glaze, mix five parts of Glazing Liquid to one part of Satin Oil Base Paint tinted to the proper color. One gallon of Glazing Liquid to one quart of Oil Base Paint is usually the right amount for the average size room.

As long as you work fast enough, some paint manufacturers recommend that you can use a Satin Gloss Latex Enamel for the glaze coat. It makes clean up a lot easier.

4   Roll on the glaze to the first 3 or 4 foot wide section. If you are using a two person team, the first person does steps # 4 and 5. The second person does step # 6.

5   Cut in your corners, base and ceiling.

FAUX PAINTING

6   Drag your combing tool from the ceiling down to the floor. It is critical that you keep your lines straight (if they are supposed to be straight that is), here. Keep combing until you are one "comb" width away from the edge of the four foot width. This is your "wet edge". Don't start this area until the next section is laid down or you will end up with obvious lap marks when the paint is dry.

Keep cleaning off your "comb" with a rag or paper toweling.

7   DO NOT STOP. Keep going until you are finished with the room. Repeat steps 4 - 6 until you are done.

Do not let the paint get tacky. Do not go back and apply more glaze if you slip up on one area. That is part of the design. Going back will darken the color in that section of the wall and be very obvious when the paint is dry.

When you get very brave at this, you may decide to use two glaze coats. The first coat is combed vertically. The second coat is applied and combed horizontally.

PROJECT: WOOD GRAINING

Virtually any smooth surface can be wood grained. That means that those composite or old formica cabinets, steel or vinyl doors, desks, wardrobes and files are all just waiting for you.

FAUX PAINTING

I recommend using, or at least starting with the Old Masters$^{(r)}$ Wood Graining Kit because no one does a better job and their wood graining tool could spell the difference between success and failure on your job.

After you become an "old pro" at wood graining you can buy other Graining Tools and special Wood Graining Rollers at many paint stores that specialize in supplies for the painting trade.

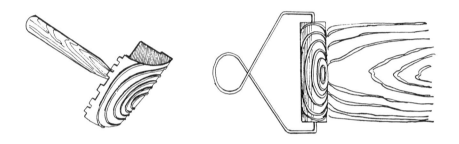

CONDITION: Pre-Painted Surface.

MATERIALS NEEDED: Paint & Stain Remover, Liquid Deglosser, Tack Rag, Old Masters$^{(r)}$ Wood Graining Kit or comparable, Alkyd Oil Eggshell Enamel Base Paint, high pigment /slow drying Stain, Satin Polyurethane.

SPECIAL EQUIPMENT NEEDED: 120 and 220 Grit Sandpaper, Natural Bristle 2 1/2" Brush, Foam Brush, Old Masters$^{(r)}$ Wood Graining Wood Graining Tool, and Artist Brush.

FAUX PAINTING

TIME REQUIRED: Five days (includes drying and curing time).

PROCEDURE:

I could just say buy the Old Masters$^{(r)}$ Wood Graining kit and follow the directions. Each kit contains a very comprehensive sixteen page brochure. These directions are included to let you read enough about the technique to see if you want to do the job before you buy the materials. One Wood Graining Kit has enough materials to cover approximately 50 square feet.

One important tip the company gives is to make a 12" X 20" practice board and practice each step before you carry out each step on your practice. This is absolutely essential.

1   Make certain that you are working in a well ventilated, dust free environment. Remove any preexisting paint or stain with a good paint and stain remover.

2   Sand the surface lightly with Medium Grade (120 - 150 Grit) Sandpaper. If you are working on an especially hard, smooth surface, like metal, cover surface with a Liquid Deglosser. All sanding strokes, and deglosser strokes must be in the direction of the grain.

3   Apply your base coat of paint with a good quality natural bristle brush. Be careful to paint in the direction of the wood grain.

4   Allow base to dry thoroughly. One day drying time is usually sufficient.

FAUX PAINTING

5   Lightly sand surface in the direction of the grain with Fine Grit (220 - 280 Grit) Sandpaper.

6   Apply first coat of stain with a foam brush.

7   Let dry completely, approximately 12 hours.

8   Apply the second coat of stain with a foam brush a small section at a time. Immediately work the stained area with the Wood Graining Tool. Use the same stroke and pressure that you would if using a squeegee. Clear up any imperfections with an eraser, or smooth them out with an Artist's Brush.

        If you do not have a Wood Graining Tool, you can "paint" in the wood grain with a variety of different sizes of Artist's Brushes.

9   Let dry for 15 to 20 minutes.

10   Gently stroke over the area with a natural bristle brush. All brush strokes must be in the direction of the grain.

11   Let dry thoroughly, approximately 12 hours.

12   Tack Rag.

13   Apply a finish coat of Satin Polyurethane.

14   Let cure for 36 hours.

GLOSSARY

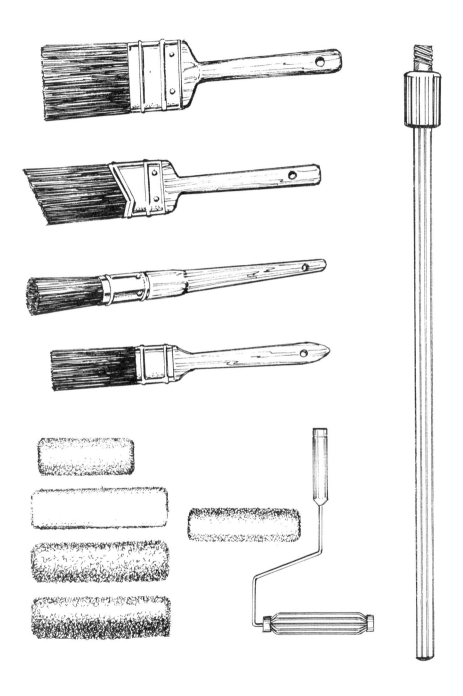

GLOSSARY

Acoustical Ceiling Tile: Sound absorbing tiles usually found in hung ceilings. Low paintability.

Acrylic: A synthetic polymer binder used in Latex Paints. Improves paint Life and color Retention. One of the signs of a premium quality paint.

Adhesion: Paint's ability to hold to surface without peeling, flaking or blistering.

Airless Sprayer: Spray equipment that uses hydraulic pressure, instead of air pressure, to atomize paint.

Alkyd Oil Based Paint: Oil based paint made from synthetic resins. Used for both interior, exterior and metal coatings. One of the signs of a premium quality paint.

Alligatoring: Paint failure with cracks appearing in a rectangular pattern.

Anti-Rust Primer: Primer with rust inhibitor additive.

Atomize: Breaking up of paint or other substance into tiny droplets.

Back Priming: Priming of the back side of exterior wood that will not be visible after installation.

Baseboard: Interior wood trim.

Base Coat: Undercoat of paint upon which other paints are applied. When wood graining, sponging, or combing, the base coat is often a contrasting color to the later coats.

Base Color: The color of the base coat.

GLOSSARY

Binder: One of three main ingredients of paint. Determines paint's performance properties: washability, toughness, adhesion, durability and fade resistance.

Bleaching: Fading of color due to ultra violet rays of the sun. Also, the use of Oxalic Acid or other bleaching agent to lighten or restore natural wood color.

Bleeding: Reappearance of old paint color or stain through new coat, necessitating use of stain kill before final coat.

Blistering: Formation of air pockets in paint caused by heat or moisture.

Boxing: Mixing of gallons of the same color paint in a larger container to assure even color throughout the job.

Bridging: The filling of surface cracks, voids and pores by paint.

Broken Color Painting Technique: Term applied to any one of many "faux" painting (hand applied, multi-colored painting) techniques.

Build Up: The accumulated thickness of coats of paint on a surface.

Casement Window: Window that opens outward like a door.

Caulking: Flexible filler for holes, joints and trim. Seals out cold and moisture; also fills gaps to provide a solid appearance.

GLOSSARY

Chair Railing: Decorative strip of wall molding about 35" above floor, designed to keep chairs from scraping the wall.

Chalking: Gradual disintegration of paint surface into a powdery substance.

Checking: Small, vertical cracks in paint.

Cissing: Splattering of a solvent on a wet paint or varnished surface for the design effect. Honest folks, some people do this.

Color Retention: Ability of paint to resist fading.

Combing Technique: Method of applying a contrasting second coat of paint, then "combing" in a design pattern into the paint by pulling a specially prepared squeegee through the paint.

Consistency: Density of paint.

Cove: A strip of wood or other material fitted into the angle between the wall and ceiling to hide cracks and prove a neater, more decorative finish.

Cracking: Breaks in paint surface.

Cross Stroke: "X" brush stroke used in broken color painting techniques.

Crown Molding: Interior, decorative wood trim at junction of ceiling and walls.

Custom Mixed Paint: Paint mixed at store to specific color selection, usually from swatches.

GLOSSARY

Cutting-In: Use of a small brush or roller to provide constant paint coverage around doors and windows, at corners, and the junction of wall and ceiling.

Deglosser: Chemical agent that takes the high sheen off of painted surface to make new coat of paint adhere better.

Deglossing: Taking the shine off glossy surfaces, such as enamel, by roughening with sandpaper or chemicals to make adhesion better for a new coat of paint.

Double Hung Windows: Vertically opening windows.

Dragging: Pulling stiff-bristled broom, brush, or comb through an outer coat to expose an under coat.

Drop Cloth: A large piece of canvas, plastic or paper designed to protect floors, furniture, and other objects from accidental splashing during paint application.

Dry Measure: Measurement of ingredients in dry not liquid form.

Dry to Recoat: Paint dry enough for next application.

Dry to Touch: Paint has dried sufficiently so that a light touch will not make finger marks.

Drywall: A large piece of gypsum covered with paper, used to finish interior walls and ceilings.

Durability: Degree to which paint resists weathering from sun, rain, wind, heat, cold, etc.

Eggshell Paint: Low luster paint finish.

GLOSSARY

Elasticity: Ability of paint to expand and contract from heat and cold without changing appearance, cracking or losing adhesion.

Embossed Wallpaper: A heavy, textured wallpaper designed to be painted. Provides a variety of patterns to wall surfaces.

Enamel: Typically a paint that dries to a hard, smooth finish. Comes in both Latex and Oil Based Satin, Flat, Semi Gloss, and High Gloss varieties. Made for both interior and exterior use.

Epoxy: A resin based paint used on non-porous surfaces. Very hard and durable, it dries by chemical action, no evaporation. Special care and training is needed to use this paint successfully.

Expanded Vinyl: A lightweight material that gives the appearance of fabric, yet is easy to apply and strip.

Extender: A lower cost additive, like clay, that extends pigment's capabilities and/or adds bulk to paint by adding density to paints consistency.

Extension Handle: Four to six foot handle that attaches to rollers and sanding pads , for use on painting and prepping walls and ceilings.

Fading: Lightening of color due to sun.

Faux Painting Techniques: General term applied to all hand applied patterning techniques such as stenciling, rag rolling, feather dusting, marbling, masking, sponging or combing.

GLOSSARY

Feathering: Light sanding of the edges of a painted area. Also a gradual lifting of the brush at the end of a stroke so as to obscure the edge.

Feather Dusting: Hand Patterning technique using the tip of a feather duster to make multiple feathered patterns on a wall. (Trust me on this one. It can really look great.)

Ferrule: The metal band that goes around a paint brush and holds the bristles in place.

Fillers: Products used to fill in cracks or holes in wood, plaster, dry wall or masonry.

Film Build: Progressive recoating to provide surface protection.

Film Thickness: Depth of coating in millimeters.

Fire Retardant Paint: Latex paints with heat resistant properties caused by the addition of silicone or other fire resistant chemicals.

Film Formation: Paint's ability to form a solid film after the evaporation of the thinner.

Finish Coat: The top coat of paint.

Flaking: Breaking away of small pieces of paint from the substrate caused by failure of paint's adhesion characteristics.

Flat Paint: A luster free paint made for both interior and exterior use.

GLOSSARY

Gel Stain: An oil based stain, applied onto wood with a rag and rubbed into wood. For inside use only.

Glaze: Semi-opaque second coat of paint used in Faux Painting: Dragging, Rag Rolling, Sponging, or Stippling.

Glaze Coat: The special Latex second coat used in faux painting.

Gloss: The reflectivity of paint. High gloss paint reflects light and highlights surface irregularities. Flat gloss paints have low reflectivity.

Grain: The natural pattern of wood.

Green Board: Specially made, water resistant board, used as an underlayment for tiles under, and around, shower stalls and baths.

Grout: A light cement mixture sealing spaces between tiles.

Hiding Power: Ability of paint to cover original surface color. Provided by pigment.

Knot: A part of the pattern of the wood. It marks the place where a branch was growing. May have to be sealed before painting or varnishing.

Lacquer: A quick drying, usually clear coating, for interior surfaces.

Latex Paint: Water based paint made with synthetic binders. Soap and water cleanup.

GLOSSARY

Laying Off: With paint it means the uniform direction of the finish stroke. With varnish, it can mean the final stroke, plus the cross stroke sometimes needed at the edge of the surface to prevent running.

Laying On Paint: The act of bringing the supply of paint or varnish from the can to the surface. Not a finishing stroke.

Leveling: Ability of paint to form a smooth coat with no brush marks.

Lining Paper: A thick, usually, cellulose impregnated paper, applied to uneven walls to provide a smooth surface for paint or paper.

Liquid Sandpaper: Chemical deglossing agent painted on hard or glossy surface to make paint adhere.

Marbling: A faux painting technique which gives the look of marble to a painted surface.

Masonry: Poured or block concrete, bricks or stone.

Masonry Paint: Special Oil or Latex Paints especially designed for use on masonry surfaces.

Masking: Covering of an area to protect it from accidental paint coverage.

Masking Tape: Paper tape used to protect non-painted surfaces from accidental painting. New grades leave no adhesive residue, when left for long periods.

Mildew: A living fungus that thrives on paint proteins and high moisture environments.

GLOSSARY

Mildewcide: Chemical agent that inhibits growth of mildew when added to paints.

Mineral Spirits: Solvent that has been distilled from petroleum.

Molding: Trim around door or window, or between floor and wall.

Mottling: A smudgy stipple made by dabbling a sponge or brush up and down.

Muriatic Acid: Commercial hydrochloric acid used to clean alkali deposits from masonry.

Mullion: Wood, plaster or metal divider between window panes.

Negative Method: Faux Painting technique in which the glaze coat is removed to expose the undercoat in a patterned design.

Oil Base Paint: Paint made with linseed or other vegetable oils. Cleans and thins with paint thinner or mineral spirits.

Orbital Sander: Machine sander with a rectangular pressure pad.

Paint: Oil or water based coating made from a combination of solvents, pigments and resins.

Paint Thinner: Water, mineral spirits, or turpentine used to clean or thin paint.

GLOSSARY

Paint Tray: Paint container for use with roller.

Particle Board: Compressed wood and glue board made into 4' X 8' sheets. For underlayment of floors to be carpeted or tiled.

Patching Compound: Plaster or vinyl paste used to fill holes and cracks in wood, plaster or drywall before painting.

Pattern Work: The general structure of the design in stenciling or other decorative painting.

Peeling: Ribbons of paint formed by paint's loss of adhesion characteristics.

Penetrating Oils: Tunge, Linseed, or Rosewood Oils used to waterproof, seal or finish wood.

Pigment: One of paint's three basic components. The finely ground particles that provide paint's color and opacity.

Polymer: In paint, a substance consisting of giant molecules formed from smaller petrochemical molecules to improve paint's binding characteristics.

Polyurethane: A very durable clear varnish used for floors, countertops and trim.

Porosity: Absorption quality of wood, masonry, etc.

Positive Method: Faux painting technique in which a second and third coat are added as part of patterning.

Primer: Oil, or Latex base coat that penetrates and seals surface to be painted.

GLOSSARY

RAGROLLER(TM): Special roller used to speed and ease the Faux Finish painting technique of rag rolling. Invented by David Campbell, New Baltimore, Michigan.

Rag-Rolling: Use of a rolled rag to apply or remove a patterned over coat, exposing under coat of paint in a variated pattern.

Retarder: A colorless gel mixed with some water-based paints to retard drying time by slowing evaporation.

Resins: Chief binding agent in paints. Synthetically produced resins are used in alkyds, acrylics and urethanes.

Roller: Cylinder shaped paint applicator formed by filling a roller cover over a roller frame.

Roller Cover: Sleeve over roller frame that provides the actual applicator.

Sash Brush: Angled or straight bristle brush especially designed for painting window sashes and moldings.

Satin Finish Paint: A paint finish that has a slightly higher sheen rate than eggshell. It is about midway between gloss and flat paint.

Scaffolding: A platform supported by a metal frame, for painting or other wall or ceiling work.

Scraper: A metal tool used to remove paint.

Sealer: A clear coat product which penetrates wood or masonry and serves as a barrier to moisture and dirt. This is essential protection for decks and concrete driveways.

GLOSSARY

Sheen: The reflective quality of paint. Often expressed as a "high" sheen rate for high gloss enamels, and a "low" sheen rate for flat paints.

Shellac: The same word is used for both the resin and the thin, clear varnish made from a mixture of this resin and alcohol.

Siding: The wood, metal or vinyl covering that provides the exterior surface of a house.

Sizing: A necessary undercoat painted on plaster or drywall before hanging wallpaper.

Skin: Drying paint slick that forms over the surface of oil base paint.

Sleeve: Roller cover.

Solvents: Paint thinners, such as water or mineral spirits. One of three main ingredients in paint.

Spalling: Deterioration of unsealed, water logged, brick and cement. It is caused by the freezing and expansion of the absorbed water, breaking off large chips of the brick or cement surface.

Spackling Compound: A soft material used to fill imperfections in plaster and drywall before painting.

Spar Varnish: Oil based exterior varnish.

Spattering: Droplets of paint that spin off when roller is used.

GLOSSARY

Sponge Coat: Glaze coat use in Faux Finishes.

Sponging: Application of contrasting Latex Eggshell or Flat Paints with a damp sponge on a Flat Latex surface.

Stain: Coloring and protective coating used on wood or cement. Soaks in, does not lay on top like paint. Important: Cement stain and wood stain are two different products. They are not interchangeable.

Stain: Also mean the accidental discoloring of a surface area by paint, scorching, mildew, etc.

Stain Blocker: Coating applied to old or discolored surface to prevent color from bleeding through new paint.

Steel Wool: Available in many grades and used for final preparation of painted or varnished surface. Area must be tack ragged carefully before painting to assure that all filaments have been removed.

Stenciling: Decorative, age-old painting technique that permits a repeated trim design using patterns cut from clear acetate.

Stippling: Use of a sharp, stiff-bristled brush, sponge or cloth, to create a pattern by exposing under coat of paint.

Strippable Paper: Wallpaper that has been specifically designed for ease of removal without water.

Stripper: Heat based, or chemical agent used to strip paint from wood and metal surfaces.

GLOSSARY

Stud Wall: A hollow, non-bearing wall made from joists and drywall.

Tack Rag: Sticky cloth used to clean final dust, sawdust, steel wool residue from surface before painting or varnishing a surface.

Tacky Surface: Slightly sticky newly painted surface caused by improper drying.

Template: The master design from which stencils are cut.

Textured Paint: A thick, premixed or powdered paint. some are designed to automatically leave a pattern. Others must be worked by hand with stiff brushes or trowels.

Thinner: One of three major ingredients to paint. In Oil Based Paints this is a turpentine or linseed oil. In Latex Paints, this is water.

Thixotropic Paint: Non-drip Alkyd, Oil Based Paint.

Tipping Off: Touching off the tips of the bristles of a brush to the sides of the paint can to make certain that there is not too much paint or varnish in the brush.

Translucent Color: Gauze-like outer coating of paint that permits you to see presence of the base coat beneath it.

Transparent Color: Color which alters the tint of the base coat beneath it, without obscuring the base color.

Trim: Decorative wood, vinyl or metal applied to surface to improve aesthetic effect.

GLOSSARY

Trim Paint: Hard enamel paint applied to trim surfaces.

TSP: Trisodium Phosphate. A strong cleaning agent used to clean and degrease surfaces before painting. In stronger solutions it can actually degloss paint. New, environmentally benign formulations of TSP are now available for use in States which restrict Phosphate use.

Tung Oil: Oil of Tung tree used in fine wood finishing paints.

Turpentine: Paint thinner made from the sap of the pine tree. Can replace mineral spirits. Although it has a pungent odor, it does not have toxic fumes.

Ultra Violet Rays: Destructive rays from the sun that prematurely discolor and age wood (Imagine what it does to human skin).

Undercoat: A layer of paint applied before the final coat of paint. This is usually applied to provide a smooth, stain free surface.

Undertoning: The soft hued, base coat that forms the foundation prior to the veins and top glazes that are applied during marbling.

UV: Abbreviation for Ultra Violet.

UV Blocker: The ingredient in a sealer, stain or paint that impedes penetration of destructive Ultra Violet Rays.

UV Coating: A coating designed to impede the penetration of Ultra Violet Rays. For exterior use. Used primarily on decks and siding.

GLOSSARY

Urethane: A durable, clear varnish. The same as polyurethane.

Varnish: A clear, usually high gloss, or semi gloss, oil based finish coat used on wood surfaces. Provides luster and protection while permitting the natural beauty of the wood grain to show.

Vehicle: Combination of binder and thinner that, when combined with pigment, creates paint.

Vinyl: A synthetic resin most often used in Latex Paint. Polyvinyl Chloride (PVC) is sometimes used in Oil Based Paint where high chemical resistance is necessary.

Viscosity: The resistance to spread or flow of paint.

VOC: Volatile Organic Content. Technically any carbon compound that evaporates under standard test conditions. For our purposes, any paint solvent except water that evaporates. VOC may be a concern to air purity standards.

VOC Paints: Paints that conform to higher air quality standards.

VOC Stains: Stains that conform to higher air quality standards.

VOC Varnishes: Varnishes that conform to higher air quality standards. These varnishes have a very low "build rate" and multiple coats are always necessary.

Volume Solids: The volume of Pigment and Binder solids expressed as a percent. The thicker the paint, the larger the percentage of Binder and Pigment by volume.

GLOSSARY

Wainscotting: A purely decorative wood facing used on the lower wall.

Wash: Tinted Clean Coat in Faux Painting.

Washability: Ability to remove dirt from paint surface without causing damage to paint.

Water Repellent: The silicone or acrylic powder used to make special "waterproof" paint for wood.

Wood Graining: Creation of a wood grain look on any surface using a combination of base coat, stain coats, and special brushes and squeegees, plus a final protective polyurethane coat.

Wood Preservatives: Toxic liquids painted on, or impregnated into wood under high pressure, to protect against insects, fungi, and rotting.

Wood Putty: A hard drying, relatively strong material used to patch holes in wood prior to painting. May be sanded, drilled, painted, or stained like the wood that surrounds it.

Wrinkling: Wrinkled paint failure caused by improper paint application. Paint was applied too thickly and the top coat dried before the bottom coat.

APPENDIX

I STAIN KILL CHARTS

Plaster & Dry Wall

PROBLEM	RECOMMENDED STAIN KILL
Ball Point Pen	Oil Base
Dark Paint Cover	Water Base
Fire Damage	Oil Base
Fire / Smoke Damage	Oil Base
Flaking	Oil Base
Graffiti	Water Base
Grease	Oil Base
High Gloss Paint	Water Base
Lipstick / Crayon	Water Base
Mold / Mildew	Water Base after removal
Nail Pops	Water Base
Oily Surface	Oil Base
Rust Stain	Water Base
Sticky Paint	Oil Base
Water Damage	Oil Base
Water Stain	Oil Base

I STAIN KILL CHARTS

Wood Surface

PROBLEM	RECOMMENDED STAIN KILL
Ball Point Pen	Water Base
Dark Paint Cover	Oil Base
Fire Damage	Oil Base
Fire / Smoke Damage	Oil Base
Flaking	Water Base
Graffiti	Water Base
Grease	Oil Base
High Gloss Paint	Water Base
Lipstick / Crayon	Water Base
Mold / Mildew	Water Base after removal
Nail Pops	Water Base
Oily Surface	Oil Base
Rust Stain	Water Base
Sticky Paint	Oil Base
Water Damage	Oil Base
Water Stain	Oil Base
New Wood Trim	Water Base

I STAIN KILL CHARTS

Cement, Masonry, Cinder Block

PROBLEM	RECOMMENDED STAIN KILL
Ball Point Pen	Water Base
Dark Paint Cover	Water Base
Fire Damage	Oil Base
Fire / Smoke Damage	Oil Base
Flaking	Water Base
Graffiti	Water Base
Grease	Oil Base
High Gloss Paint	Water Base
Lipstick / Crayon	Water Base
Mold / Mildew	Water Base after removal
Nail Pops	Water Base
Oily Surface	Oil Base
Rust Stain	Water Base
Sticky Paint	Oil Base
Water Damage	Oil Base
Water Stain	Oil Base

I STAIN KILL CHARTS

Brick

PROBLEM	RECOMMENDED STAIN KILL
Ball Point Pen	Water Base
Creosote	Alcohol Base
Dark Paint Cover	Water Base
Fire Damage	Oil Base
Fire / Smoke Damage	Oil Base
Flaking	Water Base
Graffiti	Water Base
Grease	Oil Base
High Gloss Paint	Water Base
Lipstick / Crayon	Water Base
Mold / Mildew	Water Base after removal
Nail Pops	Water Base
Oily Surface	Oil Base
Rust Stain	Water Base
Sticky Paint	Oil Base
Water Damage	Oil Base
Water Stain	Oil Base

I STAIN KILL CHARTS

Metal

PROBLEM	RECOMMENDED STAIN KILL
Ball Point Pen	Water Base
Creosote	Alcohol Base
Dark Paint Cover	Oil Base
Fire Damage	Oil Base
Flaking	Oil Base
Graffiti	Oil Base
High Gloss Paint	Water Base
Rust Stain	Oil Base
Sticky Paint	Oil Base
Water Damage	Oil Base
Water Stain	Oil Base

I STAIN KILL CHARTS

Other Surfaces

SURFACE	RECOMMENDED STAIN KILL
PVC PIPE	Water Base
NON POROUS WALL COVERINGS	Water Base
WALL PAPER	Water Base
GALVANIZED METAL	Water Base
BRASS	Water Base
CHROMIUM	Water Base
ALUMINUM	Water Base
STAINLESS STEEL	Water Base
IRON	Water Base
STEEL	Water Base
FACTORY ENAMELED METAL	Water Base
WROUGHT IRON	Water Base

II STAIN KILL BRANDS

MAJOR BRANDS OF STAIN KILLS BY CLASSIFICATION

Many of the major, full line paint manufacturers / distributors also make Oil Based and Latex Water Based Stain Kills as part of their lines. Some of these include, but are not limited to, **Ace, Bruning Paint Company, Samuel Cabot, Cook & Dunn, Custom Building Products, James B. Day, Dupont Company, Dutch Boy, Fuller-O'Brien, Gibson-Homans, Glidden, Harrison, Illinois Bronze, Kurfee's Paints, McCloskey, Minwax, Benjamin Moore, Muralo, Olympic Home Care, Pittsburgh Paints, Pratt & Lambert, Rust-Oleum, Thompson & Formby's, Tru-Test, United Gilsonite, United Solvent, Valspar, and Zehung Corp.**

The following lists include the names of some of the most experienced, specialized manufacturers and most broadly distributed, and time honored, brand names. These are not comprehensive lists, but they give you good places to start.

COMPANY   BRAND NAME

OIL BASED STAIN KILLS

Company	Brand Name
Wm. Zinsser	Kover Stain
X-I-M Products, Inc.	X Seal
Master Chem	Kilz
Mantrose Hauser	Hide'n Seal
	Maximum Hide'n Seal

II STAIN KILL BRANDS

COMPANY	BRAND NAME

WATER BASED ACRYLIC STAIN KILLS:

Wm. ZINSSER.................. Bulls Eye 1-2-3
XIM.................................... X-Out
Mantrose-Haeuser............ Ultra Maxhide
Master Chem...................... Kilz II

SHELLAC ALCOHOL BASED STAIN KILLS:

Wm. Zinsser...................... B-I-N
Mantrose-Haeuser............ Enamelac
Master Chem...................... Kilz Shellac

SPECIAL PURPOSE PAINT/ STAIN KILLS:

ANTI MILDEW

Wm. Zinsser...................... Perma White
                              Bathroom
                              Wall & Ceiling Paint

Porter Paints..................... PorterSept

III COLOR USE & SELECTION

Color is a personal choice. This book is not meant to tell you how to select the colors for your home. There are many great books on interior decorating. Almost all paint and paint and wallpaper stores have consultants on hand who can help you select the best colors. You'll also find exciting color combinations in fabric and wallpaper samples. Take the sample of your choice to any store with a color computer and you can get your paint mixed to these exact colors.

Light colors create the feeling of open, bright, spaces. Dark colors absorb light and make a room seem smaller and more intimate. Warm colors, reds, yellows, browns, and oranges, add excitement and actually make people feel warmer. Cool colors, blues, greens, lavenders and grays, open open up a room. They can actually make a room seem cooler.

Use the Color Wheel to make your paint selection.

COLOR WHEEL

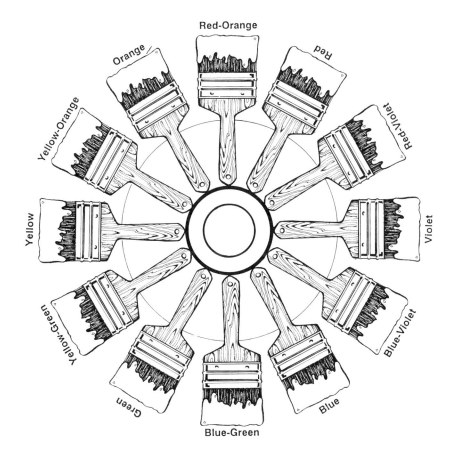

III COLOR USE & SELECTION

MONOCHROMATIC COLOR SCHEMES

Monochromatic color schemes are comprised of various shades of the same primary color. Your paint store has color strips on the basic colors. You can use these to choose to do a room in two or three different shades of blue or green, or yellow. A monochromatic color scheme is usually very restful. It gives continuity and adds a feeling of spaciousness to small, crowded areas. It is a great choice for rag rolling or sponging.

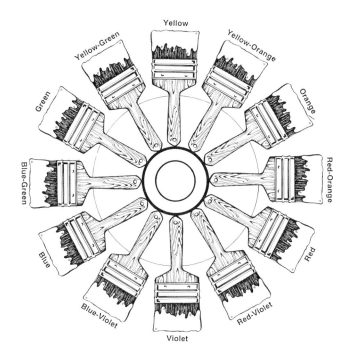

Every primary color, Blue, Blue-Green, Green, etc. is the foundation for a Monochromatic color scheme.

III COLOR USE & SELECTION

ANALOGOUS COLOR SCHEMES

Analogous Color Schemes use neighboring colors, or shades of these colors. An example would be Blue-Green, Blue and Blue-Violet. One color should predominate. Get color strips of all three colors from your paint store before deciding on your color selection.

You'll find a lot of Wallpaper designs use Analogous Color Schemes.

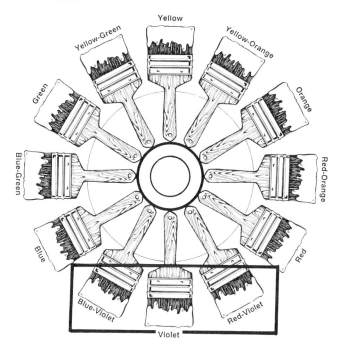

Shades of three companion colors, such as (a) Blue-Violet, Violet, Red-Violet, or (b) Green, Yellow-Green, Yellow, etc. create an analogous color scheme. You could also use: Blue, Blue-Green and Green.

III COLOR USE & SELECTION

TRIAD COLOR SCHEMES

Triad Color Schemes combine shades of three different primary colors spaced an equal distance apart on the color wheel. An example would be Green, Orange, and Violet, or Yellow-Green, Red-Orange, and Blue-Violet. Be sure to make one color and its shades predominant. The second color should be used less. The third color, just for accents.

Triad Color Schemes are always three colors, an equal distance apart. Such as Blue, Yellow, Red; or Blue-Violet, Yellow-Green, Red-Orange; etc.

III COLOR USE & SELECTION

COMPLIMENTARY COLOR SCHEMES

Complimentary Color Schemes combine colors (and shades of these colors) that are opposite each other on the color wheel. An Example would be Blue and Orange, or Green and Red. Make one of these colors the primary color and use several different shades of that color. Accent with the secondary color.

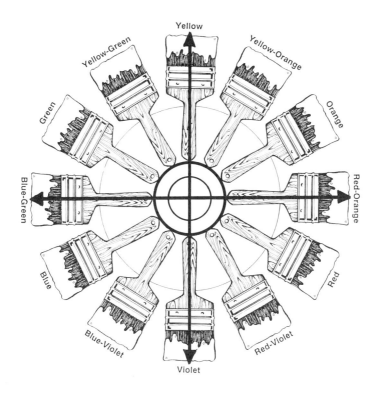

Complimentary Colors are Yellow and Violet; Blue-Green and Red-Orange, Green and Red, etc.

IV PAINT CALCULATION FORMULA

The amount of paint you need for a given project is determined by dividing the total square footage by the spread rate of the paint. Every paint is different. The average spread rate, is somewhere between 250 and 500 square feet per gallon. The following chart is one adapted from The Rohm and Haas Paint Quality Institute. Be sure to do a separate calculation for the ceiling. Remember Cabinets, etc. have shelf bottoms as well as tops. Double the amount if you are applying two coats.

PAINT CALCULATION FORMULA

1 The width of all the walls X the Height of the walls.

2 Height of each Window X the Width = Window Surface.

3 Repeat for each Window. Add total Window Area.

4 Height of Door X Width of Door = Door Surface

5 Repeat for each Door. Add total Door Area.

6 Total of Lines 3 and 5.

7 Subtract to total from line 6 from the total on line 1.

8 Divide Total of line 7 by Spread Rate = Gallons needed for each coat of paint.

V PAMPHLETS, MAGAZINES, BOOKS

PAMPHLETS

This is just a very short list of some of the many pamphlets available to the DIY'er. Almost every company in the Paint and Coatings Industry and the Hardware Industry on both the manufacturing and retailing levels is constantly at work improving "How To" information for you. Many of these are magnificent four color works that you will want to keep in your permanent files.

BASIC COATINGS: *Five Helpful Hints to a Successful Professional Image Finishing Job*
>Basic Coatings, 2124 Valley Drive, Des Moines, IA 50321

DONALD DURHAM COMPANY: *Adventures in Water Putty*
>Donald Durham Company, PO Box 804, Des Moines, IA 50304

GLIDDEN: *Paint Pointers: Finishing Floors;*
>*Interior Wood Finishes;*
>*Selecting Brushes & Rollers*
>The Glidden Company, 925 Euclid, Cleveland, OH 44114

KURFEES PAINTS: *Painting Interiors;*
Finishing Wood Furniture
>Kurfees Coatings Inc., PO Box 1093, 201 E. Market, Louisville, KY 49202

V PAMPHLETS, MAGAZINES, BOOKS

MARTIN SENOUR: *Color & Painting Techniques; Combing; Decorator's Palette, Great Decorating Ideas with Paint from Martin-Senour; Masking; Sponging*

Martin-Senour Paints, PO Box 6709, Cleveland, OH 44101

MINWAX: *Tips on Wood Finishing*

Minwax Company, Inc., Montvale, NJ 07645

BENJAMIN MOORE PAINTS: *How to Create Fantasy Finishes with Flair & Imagination; How to Prevent Moisture Damage with Moore's Waterproofing Masonry Paint*

Benjamin Moore & Co., Chestnut Ridge Rd., Montvale, NJ 07645

NDPA: *Decorating with Confidence*

National Decorating Products Association, 1050 N. Lindberg Blvd., St. Louis, MO 63132-2994

POPULAR MECHANICS: *Great Ways to Improve Your Home # 18*

Popular Mechanics, 250 W. 55th. St., New York, NY 10019

Purdy: *How to Select the Right Paint Brush; How to Select the Right Roller Cover; The Ten Commandments of Brush Care*

Purdy Handcrafted Painting Tools, 13201 N. Lombard, Portland, OR 97203

THOMPSON & FORMBY: *Formby's Workshop, Wood Care Guide*

Thompson & Formby Inc., PO Box 677, Olive Branch, MS 38654

V PAMPHLETS, MAGAZINES, BOOKS

3M: *A Guide to Respiratory Protection*
> 3 M Occupational Health & Environmental Safety Division, Building 220-3E, 3M Center, St. Paul, MN 55144

William Zinsser: *Three Great Solutions to Common Paint Problems*
> William Zinsser & Co., Inc., 39 Belmont Drive, Somerset, NJ 08873

WILSON IMPERIAL COMPANY: *Stripping Paint from Wood*
> Wilson Imperial Company, 115 Chestnut Street, Newark, NJ 07105

WOOSTER BRUSH: *How to Use Paint Applicators*
> The Wooster Brush Company, Wooster, OH 44691

MAGAZINES

Carlsen, "Sponge & Rag Painted Walls" *The Family Handyman*, 42 # 5, May 1992: 72-78.

Jenkins, Stephanie M., "3 Ways to Paint Textured Walls - HOME REPAIRS," *WORKBENCH,* 48 #1: 52.

These are both such excellent magazines that I would like to recommend the serious DIY'er not just look up back issues, but actually, subscribe to them. Here are the addresses:

The Family Handyman: Home Service Publications Inc., 7900 International Dr., Suite 950, Minneapolis, MN 55425; $17.93 per year, Outside US: $26, Canadian GST Registration #: R123771891.

V PAMPHLETS, MAGAZINES, BOOKS

WORKBENCH: KC PUBLISHING, INC., 4251 PENNSYLVANIA AVENUE, KANSAS CITY, MO 64111; $12.95 per year (6 issues); Canadian: $ 20.28 US (includes GST).

BOOKS

Charnow, Will (1991). *Paint Your House Like a Pro: Tips from A to Z on House Painting Inside & Out.* Chester, CT: Globe Pequot.

Hemming, Charles (1985). *Paint Finishes*, demonstrations by Peter Farlow; Secaucus, NY: Chartwell Books.

Innes, Jocasta (1989). *Decorating with Paint.* New York: NY: Crown

Innes, Jocasta (1987). *Paint Magic.* New York: NY: Pantheon.

McElroy, William (1987). *Painter's Handbook*. Carsbad, CA : Craftsman Book Company.

Sandreuter, Gregg E. (1988). *The Complete Painters Handbook* Emmaus, PA : Rodale Press.

Walls, Ceilings & Woodwork (1985). Alexandria, VA : Time-Life Books.

Weldon, John B. (1989). *Paint Your House Inside and Out.* Williamsburg, VA : Shepherd.

INDEX

INDEX

INDEX

INDEX

INDEX

Ask your retailer about more of Glenn Haege's books.

If your store is out of stock, turn page for Direct Order Information. Use the same form to place your name on Glenn Haege's mail list for free information on radio, audio and video programming, plus announcements of upcoming events, newletters and books.

ORDER FORM

(MHP LOGO) Master Handyman Press, Inc.
P.O. Box 1498
Royal Oak, MI. 48068-1498 USA
Telephone: (313) 544-8043

Please send me the following books by Glenn Haege:

_____ **FIX IT FAST & EASY!**   @ $14.95 each
America's Master Handyman answers the most asked "How To" questions.

_____**TAKE THE PAIN OUT OF PAINTING!**
- INTERIORS -   @ $17.95 each
Step by step answers to almost every Interior Painting problem.

_____**TAKE THE PAIN OUT OF PAINTING!**
-EXTERIORS- (March '93) @ $17.95 each
Step by step answers to almost every exterior Painting, Staining and Wood Sealing problem.

I understand that I may return any book for a full refund if not satisfied.
Name:_____
Address:_____
_____ZIP:_____

Michigan Residents: Please add 4% Sales Tax.
Shipping: $2 for the first book and $1 for each additional. We will ship to more than one address.

_____Please add me to your mail list and send free information on newsletters and future publications.

Ask your retailer about more of Glenn Haege's books.

If your store is out of stock, turn page for Direct Order Information. Use the same form to place your name on Glenn Haege's mail list for free information on radio, audio and video programming, plus announcements of upcoming events, newletters and books.

ORDER FORM

(MHP LOGO) Master Handyman Press, Inc.
P.O. Box 1498
Royal Oak, MI. 48068-1498   USA
Telephone: (313) 544-8043

Please send me the following books by Glenn Haege:

_____ **FIX IT FAST & EASY!**   @ $14.95 each
America's Master Handyman answers the most asked "How
To" questions.

_____**TAKE THE PAIN OUT OF PAINTING!**
- INTERIORS -   @ $17.95 each
Step by step answers to almost every Interior Painting
problem.

_____**TAKE THE PAIN OUT OF PAINTING!**
-EXTERIORS- (March '93) @ $17.95 each
Step by step answers to almost every exterior Painting,
Staining and Wood Sealing problem.

I understand that I may return any book for a full refund if not
satisfied.
Name:_____
Address:_____
_____ZIP:_____

Michigan Residents: Please add 4% Sales Tax.
Shipping: $2 for the first book and $1 for each additional.
We will ship to more than one address.

_____Please add me to your mail list and send free
information on newsletters and future publications.